Death in the Everglades

THE FLORIDA HISTORY AND CULTURE SERIES

Florida A&M University, Tallahassee
Florida Atlantic University, Boca Raton
Florida Gulf Coast University, Ft. Myers
Florida International University, Miami
Florida State University, Tallahassee
New College of Florida, Sarasota
University of Central Florida, Orlando
University of Florida, Gainesville
University of North Florida, Jacksonville
University of South Florida, Tampa
University of West Florida, Pensacola

University Press of Florida

Gainesville · Tallahassee · Tampa · Boca Raton

Pensacola · Orlando · Miami · Jacksonville · Ft. Myers · Sarasota

Death in the

Everglades

The Murder of Guy Bradley,
America's First Martyr to
Environmentalism

Stuart B. McIver

Foreword by Raymond Arsenault and Gary R. Mormino

Printed in the United States of America. This book is printed on Glatfelter
Natures Book, a paper certified under the standards of the Forestry Steward-
ship Council (FSC). It is a recycled stock that contains 30 percent post-
consumer waste and is acid-free.

14 13 12 11 10 09   6 5 4 3 2 1

First cloth printing, 2003
First paperback printing, 2009

Library of Congress Cataloging-in-Publication Data
McIver, Stuart B.
Death in the Everglades: the murder of Guy Bradley, America's first martyr to
environmentalism / Stuart B. McIver.
p. cm.—(The Florida history and culture series)
Includes bibliographical references and index.
ISBN 978-0-8130-2671-8 (cloth)
ISBN 978-0-8130-3442-3 (paper)
1. Bradley, Guy Morrell, 1870–1905. 2. Environmentalists—Florida—Everglades
National Park—Biography. 3. Herons—Florida—Everglades National Park.
4. Environmental protection—Florida—Everglades National Park. 5. Murder—
Florida—Everglades National Park. 6. Everglades National Park (Fla.)—
Environmental aspects. I. Title. II. Series.
GE56.B73M35   2003
333.95'83416'0975939—dc21
[B]   2003054080

Facing foreword: "The Cruelties of Fashion—Fine Feathers Make Fine Birds."
Frank Leslie's Illustrated Newspaper, 1883. Courtesy of the Historical
Association of Southern Florida.

The University Press of Florida is the scholarly publishing agency for the State
University System of Florida, comprising Florida A&M University, Florida
Atlantic University, Florida Gulf Coast University, Florida International
University, Florida State University, New College of Florida, University of
Central Florida, University of Florida, University of North Florida, University
of South Florida, and University of West Florida.

University Press of Florida
15 Northwest 15th Street
Gainesville, FL 32611–2079
www.upf.com

*To Joan
and Stu, Jan, Barbara,
Laurel, and Margery*

Contents

Foreword

Death in the Everglades: The Murder of Guy Bradley, America's First Martyr to Environmentalism is the twenty-seventh volume of a series devoted to the study of Florida History and Culture. During the past half century, the burgeoning population and increased national and international visibility of Florida have sparked a great deal of popular interest in the state's past, present, and future. As the favorite destination of countless tourists and as the new home for millions of retirees and other migrants, modern Florida has become a demographic, political, and cultural bellwether. Unfortunately, the quantity and quality of the literature on Florida's distinctive heritage and character have not kept pace with the Sunshine State's enhanced status. In an effort to remedy this situation—to provide an accessible and attractive format for the publication of Florida-related books—the University Press of Florida has established the Florida History and Culture Series.

As coeditors of the series, we are committed to the creation of an eclectic but carefully crafted set of books that will provide the field of Florida studies with a new focus and that will encourage Florida researchers and writers to consider the broader implications and context of their work. The series includes standard academic monographs, works of synthesis, memoirs, and anthologies. And while the series features books of historical interest, we encourage authors researching Florida's environment, politics, literature, and popular or material culture to submit their manuscripts as well. We want each book to retain a distinctive personality and voice, but at the same time we hope to foster a sense of community and collaboration among Florida scholars.

Death in the Everglades chronicles the demise of one of twentieth-century Florida's most enduring folk heroes. As Stuart McIver demonstrates in this fascinating book, the murder of Guy Bradley represents a milestone not only in the saga of the Everglades but also in the broader history of American environmentalism. The story of his abbreviated yet eventful life is emblematic of the struggle to tame the Florida frontier without destroying it. Born in Chicago in 1870, Bradley moved to Florida as a young boy in 1876. For a time the family lived at the Fort Lauderdale House of Refuge, but in 1892 Guy's father, E. R. Bradley, became superintendent of Dade County's fledgling school system. Three years later the elder Bradley became involved with developer and railroad magnate Henry Morrison Flagler, and in 1898 the family moved to the isolated coastal village of Flamingo.

Situated on the southeastern fringe of the Everglades, Flamingo was a flashpoint in an emerging ecological battleground that drew the Bradleys and other pioneer families into a conflict later dubbed the Plume Wars. At the turn of the century, the mass killing of egrets and other plume birds was a serious concern among the nation's growing cadre of environmentalists, especially those who belonged to the Audubon Society, a conservation organization founded in 1886.

In 1901, at the urging of Audubon Society leaders and other like-minded environmentalists, the Florida legislature enacted a bird protection law that provided for the hiring of local game wardens. A year later Guy Bradley assumed the dual role of Monroe County's game warden and deputy sheriff. For the next three years, from 1902 to 1905, Bradley matched wits and sometimes weapons with an array of plume hunters and other nefarious characters, some of whom were strangers but many of whom were friends or acquaintances of the warden or his family. In the end, Bradley was shot and killed by Walter Smith, a man he had known for nearly a decade. How this murder came about, what happened to Smith and others left behind, and how Bradley's death and the attendant controversies affected the environmental movement are intriguing questions that frame McIver's richly textured narrative. With the instincts and skills of a master storyteller, McIver—long one of Florida's most historically minded journalists—has recaptured a tale for the ages, a story of personal sacrifice and collective awakening that altered the course of the state's natural and human history. Bradley should not be forgotten, and this book should not be overlooked by anyone seeking a full understanding of how the Everglades became a treasured but imperiled place.

Raymond Arsenault and Gary R. Mormino, Series Editors

Preface

Marjory Stoneman Douglas introduced me to Guy Bradley a quarter of a century ago. It was a brief introduction, only a couple of pages about him in *The Everglades: River of Grass,* but that was enough to make me want to learn more about this little-known hero in what I felt was an important cause. The Everglades is a unique stage for many tragedies and its cast of characters a rich and picturesque one, many heroes and heroines. But its one true hero for me was the relatively obscure man named Guy Bradley.

The Everglades has been an environmental battleground for more than a century. The first great battle began to take shape in the 1880s as Americans gazed up at the skies and noticed that many species of birds they had taken for granted were beginning to vanish. And what a terrible loss it was! The beauty of the birds in flight, the sweetness of their songs, in some cases the noisy cheerfulness of their squawking.

For those sportsmen and naturalists who, led by the American Ornithologists' Union (AOU), first addressed the problem, it was easy to trace the absurdly trivial reason for their disappearance. The birds, most notably the great plume birds, the egrets and the herons, were appearing as decorations on women's hats. The fashion craze became so sweeping that by 1886 birds were being killed for the millinery trade at the astounding rate of five million a year. At that pace how long could they last?

By the final years of the nineteenth century, the plume birds had been driven down to the tip of the country's mainland, the southern Everglades. This was the place where the last great battle would have to be fought.

Around the country, state chapters of the Audubon Society began to form and to take the first steps to save what birds they could from extinction. Most of the battles, fought in the cities of the North and the Midwest, involved educating people about how serious the problem of endangered species had become; trying to persuade the women of the Gilded Age to wear less stylish hats, hardly an easy sell; lobbying legislators to restrict the manufacture of plume-decorated hats; and, finally, stopping the killing of the elegant birds whose feathers made the hats so fashionable. These battles involved time, money, and hard work, but no real hardship and certainly no physical danger.

In 1901 the AOU persuaded the Florida legislature to pass a law making the killing of birds illegal, except for game birds such as ducks and wild turkeys. The following year Guy Bradley, of Flamingo, was hired by the AOU to enforce the law in perhaps the wildest frontier in the United States, the Everglades.

Three years later Bradley was killed in the line of duty, the first lawman to die for the country's emerging conservation movement. Wrote William Dutcher, president of the National Association of Audubon Societies: "Every great movement must have its martyrs, and Guy M. Bradley is the first martyr in the cause of bird protection."

This book is the story of Guy Bradley, a soldier on the front lines of the Everglades' first major environmental battle. He was a young man still in his thirties, a husband, the father of two small sons, a boat captain, a surveyor, a farmer, a talented violinist, and, at the end, a lawman who gave his life for his cause and for the badge.

Acknowledgments

Work on this book has extended over so many years that some who deserved to be thanked are no longer with us. They will be thanked anyway. The three whose help was most essential in launching me and helping me continue on this project were Charlton W. Tebeau, author, University of Miami professor of history, and inspiration; Charlie Brookfield, Audubon warden and author; and Carl Buchheister, former president of the National Audubon Society.

Family members and descendants of the players in this American saga who were invaluable in tracing the story include Ruby Sawyer Bradley Whitlock, widow of Guy's son Morrell; Ed Smith, son of Walter Smith, who killed Bradley; Cornelia Deas, daughter of George Elliott Cuthbert; Effie (Mrs. Loren) Roberts and her son Luther "Buddy" Roberts and other members of the extended Roberts clan; and Prof. Gilbert Voss, a nephew of Charlie Pierce, childhood friend of Guy Bradley.

Audubon people on national, state, and local levels who were vital in developing the story were Alexander "Sandy" Sprunt IV, Charles Callison, Hal Scott, Dr. Bernard Yokel, Rich Paul, Dr. Stuart Strahl, Erin Petra, and John Flicker. Among the authors whose advice was helpful were, first of all, Marjory Stoneman Douglas, and Roger Tory Peterson, Peter Matthiessen, Lawrence E. Will, Robert Lacey, Oliver H. Orr Jr., Elizabeth "Sliver" Austin, Dr. Donald Curl, and Patsy West, who was in there helping me from the very start.

A diverse group of Floridians contributed in many ways: Molly Wylly, Dr. Paul George, Sandy Dayhoff, Barry Reese, Ferguson Addison, Betty Bruce, Rebecca Smith, Tom Hambright, Rodney Dillon, Dr. Joe Knetsch, Jack Stark, Mary Linehan, Dr. William Straight, Dr. Thomas Goberville, Sam Boldrick, David Kocourek, Jack Hodges, Cricket Pechstein, Michael Lister, Jim Huffstodt, Bernie Lipsky, Thomas Rossin, and old, now departed, friend Sylvan Meyer, who piloted me to a bird's-eye view of Guy Bradley's Everglades world.

Finally, my warmest thanks go to my editors, Gary Mormino and Raymond Arsenault, who with their stalwart faith in this project gave the book a boost just when it and I needed it.

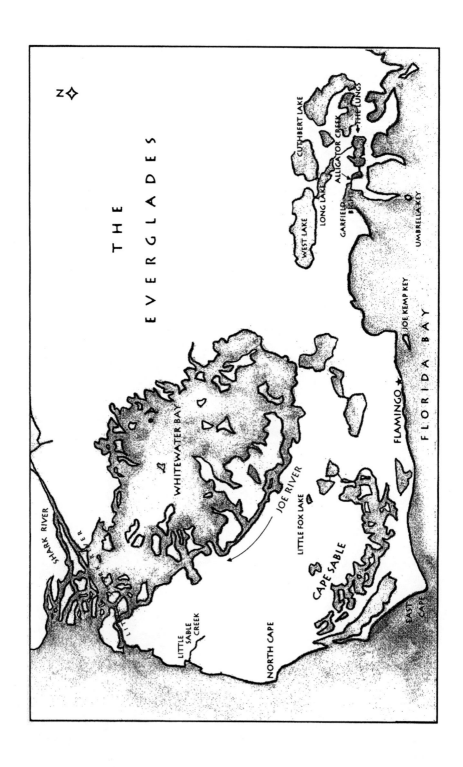

Chronology

April 25, 1870	Guy Morrell Bradley born in Chicago
1876	Bradley family moves to Florida
January 2, 1883	Guy's father, E. R. Bradley, takes job as keeper of Fort Lauderdale house of refuge
Summer 1884	Bradleys return to Lake Worth after daughter Flora dies
March 11, 1885	Cruise of the *Bonton* begins
1885	E. R. Bradley takes job as barefoot mailman
1886	American Ornithologists' Union reports five million birds killed for millinery trade the previous year
1886	First Audubon Society established
December 1889	George Elliott Cuthbert discovers Everglades rookery rich in bird life
1892	E. R. Bradley becomes superintendent of Dade County schools
1893	Captain Walter Smith arrives in Lake Worth area
1894	Henry Morrison Flagler creates major resort on Palm Beach
April 1895	E. R. Bradley joins Flagler organization
1898	Bradley and Smith families move to Flamingo
May 12, 1899	Guy marries Sophronia "Fronie" Vickers Kirvin in Key West
September 29, 1900	Guy's first son, Morrell, born in Key West
May 28, 1901	Florida passes bird protection law
1901	Steve Roberts and family arrive in Flamingo
April 1902	William Dutcher named head of National Committee of Audubon Societies

Death in the Everglades

1 The Feather Trade

IN NESTING SEASON the great rookery at the southern tip of the Everglades resembled a white cloud, a cloud in constant motion, changing its shape as noisily squawking plume birds flew in and out to bring food to newborn chicks. Far from any cities or towns, the rookery was hidden away on a small island in a blue lake surrounded by dense mangroves that made the area all but inaccessible. By the final decades of the nineteenth century it was believed the rookery, so remote it had no name, had become the last major sanctuary for eastern America's egrets and herons.

The plume birds had fled to the Everglades to escape a contagion threatening whole species with extinction. The contagion was a fashion craze. Ironically, the feathers that made the birds most attractive in breeding season made women in America's style-conscious Gilded Age more attractive the year around. Hats decorated with feathers and plumes had become the hottest items in the millinery world. And the hottest hats were those decorated with aigrettes, the nuptial plumes of the snowy egret.

Even in the Everglades the birds were not really safe from the guns of the plume hunters, who knew that somewhere deep in the Glades lay the "elephants' graveyard" of rookeries.[1] The hunters would keep looking for the last great rookery as long as the fashion market kept buying.

Then in 1886 the tide began to turn slowly in favor of the plume birds. That year, a strange event occurred on Fourteenth Street in New York City, a world as different from the Everglades as any place in America. It was a city where skyscrapers were rising to meet the needs of a population that already exceeded a million people. In the Glades what passed for buildings were mostly small shacks, some of them on stilts, and the area's sparse population was hard to gauge. Most of its settlers preferred to stay out of sight.

One February day observers near Ladies' Mile, the fashion center of the fashion capital of the country, must have wondered why a seemingly proper New York banker was eyeing so intently the stylishly dressed women parading before him.[2] Not only eyeing them, but jotting down notes about them. What was he up to? Was he a policeman or possibly a stalker?

Fishermen and big game hunters who opened their February 25, 1886, issue of *Forest and Stream* found out if they read an indignant letter to the editor headed "Birds and Bonnets." Fashionable women were not likely to read the letter from Frank M. Chapman, professional banker and amateur ornithologist. He had conducted a very thorough big-city bird count. Winter in Manhattan in the shadow of the four-story cast-iron home of R. H. Macy's department store would seem hardly the time or place to look for birds—like picking Cuba for a snowball fight. Chapman, however, knew what he was doing and just where to look. The birds he was counting, or at least parts of them, were perched atop the hats the fashion plates wore. The birds were of many sizes, shapes, and species. But they had one thing in common. They were all dead.

In his two February strolls Chapman had identified 160 different birds, among them four robins, twenty-three waxwings, nine Baltimore orioles, and one great northern shrike. What alarmed Chapman was the percentage of women whose fashion statements demanded feathers. Out of 700 hats, 542 were decorated with feathers of some kind, more than three out of four. The most elegant of the hats were decorated with aigrettes, the long, curved white plumes of egrets and herons.[3]

Behind the plumes and feathered hats lay a trail of bloody slaughter, human greed, human ingenuity, production skills, and artistry. The result was a thing of beauty that brought joy to its wearer and her admirers. The feather trade's cast of characters was a large one: in the big city, the fashion designers, millinery workers, salesmen, and retail merchants; in the swamps, marshes, and woods, the traders and plume buyers and, at the bottom of the chain, the plume hunters.

The job of the plumers, as the hunters were called, was to track the flight of the white birds, spectacular against a blue Florida sky, to the rookeries where they were nesting. Since the birds were picked off carefully one at a time, well-equipped hunters preferred relatively quiet firearms that did not alarm other birds in the rookery. Particularly popular was the Winchester .22

rifle. Some turned to the Flobert, a silent rifle developed in France for after-dinner target shooting in galleries inside the châteaux of rich noblemen, accompanied by brandy and cigars.[4]

The Everglades' skillful marksmen, more likely to turn to moonshine and chewing tobacco, relentlessly stalked their prey, knowing that at nesting time the birds in adjoining nests would not abandon their young. Patient hunters, taking their time, could "shoot out" a rookery in a day or so, leaving behind only dying baby birds. Two generations of birds would be destroyed.

Though today it seems a cruel calling, for the frontier hunter the shooting of plume birds was often the best avenue to bring home hard cash. And why would he care about the killing of birds? Plume hunting was legal, and men were expected to hunt birds and animals, whatever it took to put food on family tables.

Hats decorated with aigrettes could sell for as much as $130 in an era when unskilled workers in the millinery industry earned $10 a week for ten-hour days.[5] Plume hunters sometimes received as much as $10 for a perfect plume, as little as ten to twenty-five cents for the feathers of a lesser bird. The price extracted from America's birds, flying close to extinction, was much higher. Already doomed were the Carolina parakeet, North America's only native parrot, and the passenger pigeon, a bird that once numbered between three and five billion.

The late nineteenth century was called the Age of Extermination. Railroad passengers in the West shot buffalo from moving trains and left them to rot on the plains. Florida steamboats advertised the thrill of shooting alligators and birds on the banks of jungle rivers, then cruising on through the swaying palms to gun down more wildlife from the comfort of the boat's deck.

A whimsical travel writer of the 1870s, writing under the pen name Silvia Sunshine, cruised down the Ocklawaha River and described the sportsmen of the time:

> The trees on the banks are set closely as a cane thicket, thus obscuring all view of the surrounding country as effectually as if it were a thousand miles distant. It is to this point the sportsman resorts to indulge his propensity for killing birds, which sing songs of joy as we pass; but when wounded, their helpless bodies fall into the turbid waters—the last that is seen of them being a fluttering pinion,

signaling their sinking condition, with no one to pity or rescue. The click of the rifle is heard on every side from the hands of passengers, with the exciting remark: "O there is another alligator! Sight him quick! Kill him quick!"[6]

For centuries women, and men, had adorned their heads with feathers and plumes: knights who fought in the Crusades, Madame de Pompadour and Marie Antoinette from the elegant courts of France, and in America Seminole Indians in the hot, buggy Everglades and Plains Indians in the American West. A famous 1838 painting of Osceola by George Catlin shows him wearing an ostrich plume. Even Yankee Doodle stuck a feather in his cap.

In the final quarter of the nineteenth century the use of plumes escalated into a monstrous fad, fed by prosperous times and new advertising skills that made the product irresistible to a mass market. Explosive demand created a sudden crisis—and an alarming awareness that something had to be done.

If, as poet Emily Dickinson wrote, "'Hope' is the thing with feathers," then for a chic woman "the thing without feathers" was a hopelessly unfashionable hat. Hope, however, was the very thing that arrived in America the year young Chapman counted the winter birds of Manhattan. In the cause of bird protection, 1886 would take its place as the year the battle began to save America's plume birds.

Perhaps because of its excesses, the nineteenth century provided fertile ground for lofty moral causes—abolition of slavery, the end of imprisonment for debt, reform of penal systems, and the rise of Utopian societies. The time was right for one more cause—bird protection. And men like Frank Chapman began stepping forward to take a stand.

Another who stepped forward that pivotal year was George Bird Grinnell, editor and publisher of *Forest and Stream,* the most prestigious hunting and fishing publication in America. Taught as a schoolboy by Lucy Audubon, the widow of John James Audubon, Grinnell grew up immersed in the legend of the country's greatest painter of birds. At the school conducted in her home he saw the painter's books, his paintings, and the collection of bird skins Audubon used as models for his artwork. Incensed by the mass slaughter of birds, Grinnell in 1886 created the first Audubon Society as an adjunct to his magazine and published a brief pamphlet called the *Audubon Magazine.* Unfortunately, the first Audubon Society lasted only three years, a victim of growth so fast that Grinnell was unable to manage it and still publish his sportsman's magazine.

That same memorable year the American Ornithologists' Union (AOU), of which both Chapman and Grinnell were active members, issued a position paper as a supplement to *Science* magazine.[7] It included startling facts, strong opinions, and the text of a Model Bird Protection Law to present to state legislatures. The model law was carefully designed to protect birds of plume while heading off bitter battles over the hunting of game birds. The law exempted such favorites as waterfowl, grouse, turkey, quail, and pheasant. All other native American birds were to be protected. Recommended penalties were not severe enough to alarm legislators—"a fine of five dollars, or imprisonment for ten days, or both."

The paper's most devastating charge was that more than five million birds were being killed annually for the millinery trade in the United States alone the previous year. Among the supplement's horror stories were: 40,000 terns killed in a single month near Philadelphia; 11,018 bird skins bought by a northern dealer in one three-month trip to the South Carolina coast; 70,000 birds supplied to New York dealers in a four-month period from a single village on Long Island; a contract issued by a Paris millinery firm for the delivery of 40,000 or more birds at forty cents apiece from Cobb's Island, Virginia.

In 1886 a small settlement on the shores of Lake Worth, Florida, took the name Palm Beach for its new post office. It would become America's premier winter resort for the very wealthy and a place where the state's hunters might for the first time see the high-fashion hats their backwoods enterprise had produced. That same year a fifteen-year-old boy from Lantana, a town just across the lake from Palm Beach, made a small contribution to the five-million total of birds: four white herons, one Louisiana night heron, a wood ibis, a blue heron, and eight American egrets.[8]

Seventeen years later the boy would become a bird warden, charged with enforcing the AOU's model law in the most precious rookery still remaining in the United States. His name was Guy Bradley.

2 The Letter

IN EARLY MAY 1902, Guy Morrell Bradley, boat captain, surveyor, fiddler, husband, and father, waited anxiously for the most important letter he would ever receive. The letter would travel more than a thousand miles, from New York, America's largest city, to Flamingo, Florida, a wild, primitive fishing village hidden away at the tip of the Everglades. Guy knew the pathway the letter would take, by train from New York to Miami, by schooner to Key West, then by Flamingo's mail boat captained by Guy himself. It was all in the family. Guy's father was Edwin R. Bradley, postmaster of the little village named years earlier for the spectacular birds that had nested there until plume hunters drove them away.

Delivering the mail was a Bradley tradition. Guy's grandfather Asa had invented mail distribution boxes used for decades in Chicago, and E. R., his father, had developed South Florida's "barefoot route" for delivering the mail along the coast between Palm Beach and Miami. E. R. Bradley and Guy's older brother, Louis, had beach-walked their way into legend as barefoot mailmen. Guy, sickly as a youth, had never been strong enough to handle the grueling route by the sea.

But there was another family tradition far more important to Guy—law enforcement. As a child in Chicago, Guy had heard family stories about other Bradleys who made names for themselves in police work—Uncle Alexander, a Cook County sheriff, and Uncle Cyrus, a chief of police.[1]

Now thirty-two, his sickly phase far behind him, Guy had developed into a sturdy, muscular young man, strong enough and motivated enough to pursue the new career that by May of 1902 loomed as a very real possibility. With a wife and a little boy to support, he waited anxiously for a letter that would offer him a steady salary and the chance to be a lawman, as deputy sheriff for Monroe County and warden for the AOU.

Late in April, author Kirk Munroe had sailed into Flamingo to visit his old friends the Bradley family and to talk in particular with Guy. Munroe, a friend of Edwin and Lydia Bradley for more than two decades, had known Guy and Lou since they were children. Edwin was the Cape Sable agent for the Model Land Company, one of many enterprises owned and operated by Henry M. Flagler, the railroad and hotel tycoon who was busy developing the east coast of Florida from St. Augustine to Key West.

A founding vice president of the Florida Audubon Society, Munroe had come to Flamingo on a mission. The previous year William Dutcher, New York insurance executive and AOU activist, successfully lobbied the Florida legislature to pass the AOU's model law outlawing the killing of plume birds. Now from his busy Manhattan world Dutcher, who wouldn't have known sawgrass from cattails, faced the task of finding a warden qualified, competent, and brave enough to enforce the law in the Everglades, the Florida Keys, and the Ten Thousand Islands. In particular, the warden would have to protect a legendary nesting ground that by 1902 bore the name Cuthbert Rookery.

The Florida Audubon Society gave the task of finding a warden to patrol Florida's most crucial area to Kirk Munroe, a Coconut Grove resident with impressive credentials. By the 1890s he had become America's most popular author of books for boys. He was also a dedicated outdoorsman who knew his way around the wilderness country the warden would have to patrol. And he was a man who made things happen. While living in New York, he had founded the American Canoe Association, the New York Bicycle Club, and the League of American Wheelmen. After he moved to Coconut Grove, he and Ralph Munroe, a close friend who bore the same surname, founded the Biscayne Bay Yacht Club.[2]

Kirk's wife, Mary, the daughter of a popular British novelist, Amelia Barr, was an even more aggressive booster of the cause. When she saw women wearing hats with plumes in the ritzy hotels that Flagler was bringing to South Florida, she simply walked up to them and yanked their hats off. Since the large hats of those days were pinned to the wearers' hair, Mary Munroe's zeal provoked shrieks of pain and angry exchanges but probably very few conversions.

Kirk knew Guy had been a plume hunter as a teenager, but that could be an advantage, he reasoned. Who but a reformed plume hunter would know the ways of other plumers? The key word was "reformed," and Kirk was satisfied that Bradley's plume hunting days were behind him. He was now thirty-two, a maturing married man with a nineteen-month-old son and a thinning hairline that accentuated his seriousness of manner. Guy was a hard worker, a man who farmed and fished and hunted. He was the skipper of the *Pearl*, the Bradley family's forty-foot, two-masted sharpie, used to carry produce, charcoal, and mail between Flamingo and Key West, the Monroe County seat some sixty-five miles to the southwest. In addition, Guy served visiting sportsmen as a fishing and hunting guide. But now, with a family to support, he wanted a job that paid him a regular salary.

Munroe's letter recommending Bradley for the job painted a terrifying picture of the plight of the birds:

> At Cape Sable I found the paradise of plume hunters and the purgatory of birds. The latter, driven from haunt to haunt all over the state, have at last reached the uttermost limit of mainland territory, and to it the hunters have followed them. There dwells in a state of constant terror the last surviving flock of flamingo known to exist within the boundaries of our state; they number nearly one thousand birds and are wonderfully beautiful to look upon. There, too, are roseate spoonbills, egrets, wood ibis and many other species in sadly diminished numbers, but still numerous enough to delight the heart of an ornithologist or bird lover. But alas, the relentless plume hunter has followed them even to this remote sanctuary and the reported destruction of bird life last month is heart sickening. The utter extermination of these beautiful remnants can only be averted by the prompt appointment of a resolute game warden and a rigid enforcement of existing laws.

Munroe went on to detail the qualities he felt a warden had to have. The warden, he wrote, must "be a resident, well acquainted with local conditions, a strong, fearless man and one fully alive to the value of bird protection, also he must be not only willing but anxious to serve." Guy Bradley, he wrote, was a man who met his requirements, "a sturdy, fearless fellow, filled with a righteous indignation against the wretches who, in open defiance of all laws, are using every effort to kill off the few remaining birds of that section, and he is anxious to be invested with authority for the protection of those that still remain."

Munroe urged the society to take "the promptest possible action," contending that another season would doom the Cape Sable flocks to destruction. He also urged "a certain remuneration" for Bradley, "for he is a poor man and would be obliged to cover much territory at a great expense of time."

Dutcher wasted little time. His letter, mailed to Guy on May 6, offered him a year-round job at $35 a month, with an additional $25 a month for his brother for the five-month plume hunting season. Guy's $420 annually was $20 more than his father had earned a decade earlier as superintendent of the Dade County school system.

On May 15, 1902, just nine days after Dutcher's letter had been mailed from New York, Guy replied to the chairman of the organization fighting to save America's magnificent wading birds:

Mr. Dutcher:

Yours of May 6 received. The plume season is from Jan. 1 to June 1, during which time I will need an assistant. I can take position for $35 per month, and I can get a assistant for $25 per month for 5 months. Will go to Key West & get the appointment as warden.

Bradley

A happy Guy Morrell Bradley was embarking on a new career. Tragically, it would prove to be a brief one.

3 A Veritable Tropical Paradise

FIVE YEARS AFTER the bloody and tragic Civil War ended, Guy Morrell Bradley was born into an America surging with a powerful unleashed drive toward the western plains and the mountains beyond. His place of birth on April 25, 1870 was the bustling midwestern metropolis of Chicago, destined to become the railroad hub of western expansion and the nation's grain broker and distribution center. Poet Carl Sandburg would later call it "Hog Butcher for the World."

The Bradleys, whose ancestors came to America on the second voyage of the *Mayflower* and settled in Vermont,[1] had strong roots in Chicago. Guy's father, Edwin Ruthven Bradley, was born there in 1840, just seven years after its incorporation as a village. At least two members of the family held high positions in law enforcement, and Guy's grandfather Asa, a civil engineer, was Cook County's first surveyor. Later Asa worked for the Chicago post office, a considerable contrast to the primitive "barefoot route" Edwin would later establish on the southeast Florida coast. When Edwin was a small boy, Asa took a brief fling at the Gold Rush, venturing west to California in 1849.

The restlessness that Asa displayed as a Forty-Niner surfaced as a recurring trait in his son. Edwin never stayed long at any place, or at any job. Guy's father had hoped to be a doctor, but his medical studies were interrupted by the Civil War, in which he served in the U.S. Navy as a master's mate. Dark-haired and dark-complexioned, Edwin was a small man, five feet six, weighing only 120 pounds. Shortly after the war Edwin married Lydia Phillips in the First Baptist Church in Chicago. Born in London, she had emigrated to Chicago at an early age. A cultured woman, she displayed a considerable talent for music. But the most notable feature of Lydia's personality was a kindliness that some had described as saintly.[2]

Guy was only a little over a year old when Mrs. Patrick O'Leary's cow, the story goes, kicked over a lighted lantern in a barn. The Great Chicago Fire destroyed 17,450 buildings and left 90,000 of the city's 300,000 citizens homeless. From the blackened timbers a new Chicago arose. The Bradley family, however, was not around to see it. In 1876 E. R. Bradley decided to celebrate the United States Centennial by moving his family from a major American metropolis complete with thriving businesses, schools, churches, stores, restaurants, and hotels to a land populated by wolves, panthers, bears, snakes, alligators, and mosquitoes, a torrid land where Indians, sometimes hostile, roamed through forests and prairies and swamps. It was a land without schools or churches, all too often without laws or governments. Bradley ignored the advice "Go west, young man." Instead he went south, like a migrating bird in winter, to a land called Florida.

E. R. Bradley was a child of the city. He did not understand what he was doing—to himself, his wife, his sons, Louis, age eight years, Guy, age six, or his daughter, Flora, just three years old. The Bradleys headed first for central Florida, an area best reached in those days by steamboat on the St. Johns River.

The Bradleys settled briefly at Maitland, then moved eastward to Turkey Creek, not far from a large coastal lagoon named Indian River. At Turkey Creek E. R. Bradley came under the spell of an eloquent storyteller who had just returned from the Lake Worth country still farther to the south. It was "a veritable tropical paradise," he told Bradley.[3] The winds off the ocean, he said, kept the temperature comfortable for most of the year. The woods were filled with game, the lake and ocean teemed with fish. Lovingly he described the fertile soil on Hypoluxo Island in Lake Worth. Sweet potatoes grew profusely with little farming skill needed. Bradley was proving to be an erratic provider for his family. The island just might be the answer to his problems.

In the winter of 1877 the Bradleys bought a small schooner, loaded it with all their household goods, and sailed south for Hypoluxo Island, a ninety-mile voyage mostly through the protected waters of the Indian River. South of the Jupiter Lighthouse they steered their boat into Lake Worth. Before them lay a blue lagoon bordered by rich subtropical plant growth and dotted with small islands.

On one of these islands, near the inlet, they found a small, primitive shack. It had been the home of Jesse Malden, the lake country's first plume hunter.[4]

He had arrived at the lake in 1874 from a small Georgia town and was followed shortly by William Butler, who collected specimens of birds and animals for the University of Rochester. On Big Pelican Island, where Malden had built a second home, he and Butler located a rookery that contained virtually every kind of wading bird known to southern Florida. Long, narrow, and rocky, the island was blanketed in the spring of 1874 by nesting birds, herons of all kinds, ibis, pelicans, cormorants, anhingas, and magnificent frigate birds.

Malden cleaned out the rookery. He killed only plume-bearing herons, but the deafening roar of his gun frightened the other birds away. They never returned, moving their nesting place to a cypress swamp to the west. The next spring Malden tracked them to their new rookery and shot it out, too.

Fortunately for the Bradleys, and for the birds in the area, Malden was preparing to take a job as keeper of the Gilbert's Bar House of Refuge at St. Lucie Rocks, about thirty-five miles to the north near the St. Lucie Inlet. The Bradleys moved into Malden's home on Big Pelican Island.

The year the Bradleys came to Florida, the United States Life Saving Service began building a series of five "houses of refuge" for sailors shipwrecked along the desolate lower east coast of the state. Except for little pockets of pioneers along the shores of Lake Worth and Biscayne Bay near the mouth of the Miami River, the coastline was as bare of white settlement as the land that greeted Spanish explorers in the sixteenth century. Sailors wrecked along the southeast coast were in danger of starving or dying of thirst if they failed to salvage food or water from their ships. The keeper's job was not to plunge into the pounding seas of the Atlantic Ocean to rescue drowning sailors. Rather it was to provide a refuge for those who made it safely to shore, giving them shelter, hot food, water, warm blankets, and a place to sleep after their ordeal.

Contact with Malden was filled with omens both good and bad for the Bradleys. As the lake country's first fiddler, Malden pointed the way toward Guy's later fascination with the violin. As a keeper of a house of refuge, he made Edwin aware of a salaried job that would bring great sadness to the family. And as a plume hunter, he introduced the Bradleys to a frontier reality. Killing birds was one of the few ways a South Florida pioneer could bring cash into the home.

In early April of 1877 Guy and Lou met another lad who would become their best friend in the lake country. His name was Charlie Pierce, and like them he had been born in Illinois. The restless Edwin Bradley had decided he wanted to live in the southern end of Lake Worth. He acquired land at Lotus Cove, in today's Lantana, just across the water from Hypoluxo Island. Since he needed time to collect enough driftwood to build his house, he rented space in the home of Hannibal Pierce, Charlie's father, until he could finish construction. It was a cozy arrangement, a total of twelve people jammed into an eighteen-by-twenty-four-foot house with one room downstairs and an attic above. The dwelling was modest, but its site, the eastern waterfront on Hypoluxo Island, would later become home to Consuelo Vanderbilt, the duchess of Marlborough.

All through that summer Charlie, Lou, and Guy were kept busy each day digging sweet potatoes, chopping wood for the cook fire, and fishing for food.

"The boys," Charlie later wrote in his lengthy manuscript about pioneer life in South Florida, "were not so fond of cutting wood and digging potatoes under a hot summer sun, but the fishing—well, that was a different story. It was fun and sport no matter how necessary it might be to their food supply."

Beyond the big swamp to the west of their area lay flat woodlands that Charlie described as "a hunter's paradise." There Charlie, who was twelve, took Lou and Guy on their first plume hunt in the spring of 1877.

"Louie was only nine years old and small for his age but he was all 'grit,'" Charlie wrote. "Guy was seven and was of no use at all to Louie except to keep him company while out after something to eat. Guy would follow along behind the little hunter and when there was no game would entertain his brother with his whistling. He was good at that and could whistle any tune he had heard once or twice."

The buyer to whom the boys sold their plumes was Captain James A. Armour, keeper of the Jupiter Light. He paid them twenty-five cents a plume. Charlie found the same price was being paid at the settlement at the mouth of the Miami River. He was much impressed when he once saw an Indian arrive at William Ewan's Miami store with seven hundred snowy egret plumes for sale.

In February 1878 the Spanish brig *Providencia,* bound for Cadiz, washed ashore on the barrier island east of Hypoluxo. The brig was loaded with coconuts from Trinidad. H. F. Hammon and Will Lainhart claimed the wreck and proceeded to sell the coconuts to other settlers on the island for two and a half cents apiece. A wild orgy of coconut planting would transform the island in less than a decade into a land of palm trees and earn it its first official name, Palm Beach.

In December the Bradley family's fourth child, Rose, was born, followed two years later by another daughter, Maggie. The Bradleys, like all the other pioneers in the area, farmed, and Lou and Guy were given the task of catching fish and hunting game for the dinner table. In a pioneer home a boy had to grow up quickly. As Charlie Pierce wrote, "The gun, fishline, net and the ocean beach were the sources from which we obtained our food and whatever else we needed. In fact, if a Florida cracker was not a good hunter, he was worthless in all other ways."

Not surprisingly, the head of the Bradley household leaped at the opportunity to take a government job as keeper of the Fort Lauderdale House of Refuge, starting on January 2, 1883. It would be a lonely job in an isolated place, exposed to the hurricanes and gales that swept in from the ocean, far removed from the comfort of nearby neighbors. Still, in a land where cash was scarce, there would be a regular payday for the Bradley household. E. R.'s salary would be four hundred dollars a year.

Facing the Atlantic Ocean, the house was located on a barrier island just north of the site of the third Fort Lauderdale, built in 1839 during the Second Seminole War. All five of the houses of refuge were constructed to the same basic design, a fifty-four-by-twenty-five-foot rectangle, built sturdily to withstand even hurricane-force winds. Farther from settled areas than any of the other houses of refuge, the Fort Lauderdale station was considered the most forlorn, the most desolate of all the refuges. A government form asked, "What is the number of male inhabitants between the ages of fifteen and fifty-two years within three miles of your station?" The retiring keeper, Washington Jenkins, wrote, "None."

When the Bradleys arrived at Fort Lauderdale, they found Jenkins deathly sick, too weak even to walk. He had to be carried to the boat that brought the Bradleys to the station. Bradley was the first keeper required to fill out a logbook. He never recorded barometric readings, since the government neglected to supply him with a barometer. The thread that ran most strongly through his log was a continuing problem with the station's water supply. His cistern leaked, so even a heavy rain meant fresh water for only a short period of time. As a result, the Bradleys used a well that lay near the house. The well might have been the key to Jenkins's health problems—and to the problems that assailed the Bradley family.

That first winter, Lou went back to Hypoluxo to visit Charlie, but Lou was sick much of the time. "His face was puffed and colorless and his fingernails were blue," wrote Charlie. "He wanted to sleep all the time." On another hunting trip Guy came with them but "was sick and lay in the bow of the canoe, sleeping all the time until we stopped." Wash Jenkins, Lou, Guy, and Flora all were seriously afflicted, but for reasons not known Edwin and Lydia Bradley appeared to have escaped the problem. To make life at the station even more difficult, food seemed always in short supply, partly because the sandy beachfront soil was not conducive to growing vegetables.

In the spring Charlie sailed down to see his friends again. He tied up his boat at the landing on New River Sound. He was shaken to learn that both Guy and Flora were desperately sick. A few minutes after Charlie arrived, little Flora died. In his memoir Pierce wrote: "The workmen engaged in repairing the station made a coffin and she was buried the next day under a wide-spreading sea grape tree. Guy swelled up so badly he could not walk. I carried him to the graveside."

That summer a saddened Edwin Bradley resigned as keeper and moved back to the Lake Worth country. What had caused the strange sickness that afflicted so many at the house of refuge? A contagious infection? Possibly a contaminated or even a poisoned well? And why did it affect some people and not others? No one has ever solved the mystery.

The return to the shores of Lake Worth reunited the boys with their friend Charlie, who at nineteen was three years older than Lou, five years older than Guy. Still, the sadness from the death of Flora lingered over the Bradley household and the illness that had struck Guy left him frail and sickly for more than a year.

Charlie, always a busy operator, wasted no time in bringing the Bradley boys back into his life. In the early winter of 1885 he invited them to join him on a three-week plume hunt into a large swamp west of Lantana. Plume hunting, which was legal, came naturally to this group of footloose teenagers.[4]

Adventure lay ahead, and they were eager to go. On the other hand, for a three-week hunt Guy's strength was still something of a question mark. He was game to try to keep up with the older boys. But on the first day out, helping to push their boat up an incline proved too difficult for him.

"Here Guy went back on us," wrote Charlie. "Said it was too heavy a load for him and he could not stand it. Well, I guess it was. Guy had been sick for some time and was still rather small and puny." For most of the rest of the trip Guy carried only small items and was not active in the hunting.

The boys rated the plume hunt only a "fair success." Charlie sold his plumes to Steve Andrews, the London-born keeper of the Orange Grove House of Refuge, at today's Delray Beach. Buyers like Andrews were scattered around South Florida. They resold plumes to trading posts or shipped them north to their eventual destination, the millinery factories in New York City. Andrews paid Charlie twenty-five cents for a white egret's plume, ten cents for a plume of the great blue heron—or 'eron, as Cockney Steve called it.

"As the long white plume feathers sold by the ounce at $20 an ounce, it is plain that one would have to kill eighty birds in order to obtain one ounce of plume feathers," wrote Charlie. "They were more valuable than gold, and nearly as hard to obtain in any quantity."

For the boys it had been a great adventure, a lark, capped with a small profit at the end. And for all three it served as a training session for a much more elaborate plume hunt that would come later, a carefully organized and highly professional expedition in concert with one of the legends of the plume trade—the Old Frenchman.

It isn't clear whether his name was Alfred LeChevalier or Jean Chevalier or Jean Chevelier.[5] His name was shrouded in confusion, possibly the result of Cracker unfamiliarity with the French language. Whichever it was, he left his stamp on the region. His name appears in at least two places, Frenchman's Creek in St. Petersburg and Chevelier Bay in the Ten Thousand Islands. Even a company was named after him, the Chevelier Company, which would later hack the first paved road, the Tamiami Trail, across the Everglades.

Little is known of Chevelier's youth. Even the earliest accounts refer to him as "the Old Frenchman." On occasion he reminisced fondly about Paris, but whether he lived there or merely visited is not clear. The 1881–82 directory of the United States National Museum listed four bird specimens from Labrador donated by "A. Lechavalier, Naturalist and Taxidermist." He was located then on St. Mary's Street in Montreal. He is described as a "purveyor" for museums, colleges, and universities in Canada and foreign countries. He is credited with "Four First Prizes and Two Diplomas."

The first official record of the man in Florida is a deed written in French in Montreal on October 28, 1880, signed by A. Lechavalier and then recorded on March 16, 1881, in Tampa. The document establishes the Frenchman's ownership of 120 acres of land at Maximo Point, St. Petersburg. The purchase price was $1,800, a sizable amount of money for the times.[6]

Why did he pay so much for Maximo Point? John Bethel, who had come from the Bahamas, knew the answer. Variously described as a shipbuilder, mariner, and turtler, Bethel was one of the earliest settlers on Big Bayou, not far from Chevelier's property on the Pinellas Peninsula. As a hunter, and apparently a mighty one known to wipe out large numbers of marauding bears, wildcats, and panthers, Bethel had developed a clear, concise philosophy of hunting. He killed animals only when they threatened his stock or when he was hungry. He was incensed at the systematic slaughter of birds by plume hunters. In 1915 he wrote a small book titled *Bethel's History of Pinellas Peninsula*. He hit hard at Chevelier:

> Our section was full of game for a long time after the [Civil] war, and there would be plenty of game now if it had not been for the murderous guns in the hands of the brainless pothunters that slaughtered everything that had hair and feathers on it. There were plume and song birds of every description that the Creator had placed here to beautify and adorn Man's Paradise, but the lawless marauders just about destroyed everything that came in reach of their powder and lead.
>
> The worst scourge that ever came to Point Pinellas was one Chevelier, a Frenchman from Montreal, Canada, who located just west of Point Maximo for the purpose of killing birds for their plumes, feathers and skins. . . . Two of Chevelier's agents, Pocket and Tetu, told me that one season they got 11,000 skins and plumes.

This was the man the Bradley boys would meet, the man Charlie Pierce would work with across the summer.

In the winter of 1885 the Frenchman was living with the family of William Wagner on the Miami River. He learned that Charlie Pierce was operating a family boat called the *Bonton,* a twenty-eight-foot sloop with a seven-foot beam and a cabin big enough to give Chevelier room for himself and his three-man team, plus covered space for his taxidermy work. Pierce came to terms with the Frenchman for a lengthy bird-hunting trip along the Atlantic and Gulf of Mexico coasts of Florida.

Guy and Lou listened intently as Charlie told them about the bird-hunting expedition of a lifetime. Then the three of them put together a plan whereby the Bradley boys could accompany the *Bonton* on the first leg of the voyage, the territory between Lake Worth and Biscayne Bay. From there on it would just be Charlie, the Frenchman, and two of the Wagners. Since smaller boats would be needed for ventures back into shallow, narrow creeks, Charlie brought a canoe, the *Falcon,* and Lou and Guy a larger boat, the *Ibis.*

On March 11, 1885, the cruise of the *Bonton* began.

Since all three boys were suffering from "hard colds," their first stop was at Dr. R. B. Potter's office. There they acquired medical supplies, principally laudanum and quinine. At E. M. Brelsford's store they bought kerosene, vinegar, cocoa, onions, and fishhooks.

Not until they reached the Hillsboro Inlet on the third day did they find any concentration of plume birds. They sailed on through the inlet, anchored the *Bonton,* and resorted to their smaller boats to seek out birds. At Lettuce Lake, named after the aquatic plant called water lettuce, they saw plume birds returning to their nests.[7] They were able to shoot eight of them and vowed to find their nesting place the next day.

Cruising up Cypress Creek, they encountered wondrous sights. Wrote Charlie: "Here the creek banks are lined with tall and stately cypress trees, some of them as much as seven feet thick at the base, growing very close together, and all covered with a heavy drapery of grey Spanish moss. It was the wildest, loneliest, and at the time the most beautiful sight we had seen on any of our hunting trips."

Around a bend in the creek they found a small island. It was the home of the nesting plume birds. The three boys immediately started to shoot. "About three o'clock," Charlie wrote, "we had cleaned it all up." Lou had killed seven white herons, Charlie six white herons and one egret, and the future Audubon warden two white herons and one wood ibis.

They continued up the creek, and at sunset they again saw birds flying overhead on their way back to nests still farther to the west. The boys shot at them as they flew by. Charlie and Lou between them killed eight little blue herons and three white herons. Guy shot one white heron and a blue heron so undersized it had no plume. It was still hard for him to keep up with the older boys.

The following day the heavy going through dense growth both in the water and on land took its toll on Guy. "Guy is not at all well and I expect we will have to wait for him to rest on the way," wrote Charlie, and his fears appear to have been justified. The fourteen-year-old hunter had to stop about every half mile or so.

Guy still had trouble keeping up with them the next day. When they were within a mile and a half of the camp where they had left their boats, Lou and Charlie told Guy to go on ahead and take his time, resting any time he wanted to. This could spare him the embarrassment of stopping the caravan at such frequent intervals. About an hour later the older boys followed.

Suddenly they heard the sound of Guy's gun. Assuming he had fired as a signal, they hurried forward to find him. But they did not see him along the way. Ahead they saw the white tents of the camp. Still no sign of Guy.

Lou and Charlie rushed toward the camp. There was Guy, sitting on the ground with a big grin on his usually serious face. At his feet lay a dead turkey hen. It was the first wild turkey he had ever killed—no small feat, since the wild turkey is a wily foe for any hunter.

Soon, though, it was time to move on to the Miami River, where the Old Frenchman would be waiting. As they sailed south in the Atlantic, they passed by the Fort Lauderdale House of Refuge, where little Flora Bradley had died. At midafternoon they passed the Biscayne House of Refuge, Charlie's home when his father, Hannibal, had been keeper of the house. They cruised on through Norris Cut into Biscayne Bay and on Sunday entered the mouth of the Miami River and sailed three miles up to the home of William Wagner, set in an orange grove. Waiting there for them was Chevelier, a man of uncertain age and uncertain command of the English language.

Charlie later described his speech as "a sort of Pigeon English which is very amusing to listen to." The Frenchman called the Pierces' boat the "Bongton."

Despite his reputation on the west coast, the boys found nothing sinister about Chevelier. Why should they? To the boys, plume hunters themselves, he appeared a harmless old eccentric, worth no small number of laughs.

It was soon apparent to all that the Old Frenchman would be handicapped on the trip by the lingering effects of a serious hand injury. In the fall of 1884 his shotgun had fired accidentally while he was loading it and blasted a hole through the middle of his right hand. He was rushed to Key West, where a bizarre medical procedure took place. That is, if Pierce's account is an accurate one. Charlie wrote that "doctors cured the wound by taking the bones from three of his fingers and using them to fill the hole in the palm of his hand." As the time for the big plume hunt neared, Chevelier was still unable to use his right hand. He could shoot only by resting his gun over his right elbow.

On the trip Wagner's son William would serve as a man-of-all-work, while his grandson, seventeen-year-old Henry, would become the trip's taxidermist. Pelican skins were to be the main object of the trip; egret feathers were only the secondary target. They were also to seek cormorant skins, plus whatever birds of interest they might encounter.

"Mr. Chevelier has a market for all of them in Paris," wrote Charlie. "He gets fifty cents for the pelican skins, twenty-five cents for sea swallows and least terns, ten dollars for great white herons and twenty-five dollars for flamingo skins. Great white herons are scarce, and flamingos more so. If it was not for that we would soon make the old man rich."

The start of the hunt was still five days away. The boys tried moving upriver in their smaller vessels but soon encountered the Miami River rapids. They carried the boats around the rapids and cruised on out into the Everglades. Unfortunately, Guy became sick that afternoon. The next morning he was still sick, so Charlie gave him ten drops of the painkiller laudanum, a tincture of opium. Guy went into a sleep so long and so deep that Charlie became frightened. Then, just before dark, Guy woke up. He told Lou and Charlie he felt better. The next day he was strong enough to join his group for a visit to a nearby rookery where he killed eight plume birds.

Finally preparations were complete for the venture, and the *Bonton* sailed south to the Arsenicker Keys. The Bradley boys cruised along with the lead boat. One morning Chevelier stayed on board while the others went to one of the islands to shoot birds. They fired a few times, then heard the Frenchman angrily calling to them. He was holding his hat in his hand and pointing to it.

"The best you lookout," he said indignantly, "some shot come str-raight on my hat."

The next day, as they sailed into Card Sound, Chevelier talked about France: "The time a man sees Paree, 'tis ready to die."

Reluctant to end the adventure, Lou and Guy sailed with the *Bonton* on down to Key Largo. There they saw their first flamingo. After breakfast the next day, they faced up to reality. It was time to sail back home, time to start the dangerous ocean voyage to the lake country and their home in Lantana a hundred miles to the north. Guy had had his troubles, but he weathered the trip. And in most cases he finally kept up with the big boys.

4 The Cruise of the *Bonton*

AHEAD FOR THE *Bonton* and its crew lay the Florida Keys and the island city of Key West. A chain of nearly a thousand rocky islands, most of them small, the Keys stretched from Biscayne Bay to the Dry Tortugas in the Gulf of Mexico, a distance of roughly two hundred miles. The beauty of the blue and green water, ever changing beneath the play of the relentless Keys sun, masked a treacherous seascape for the boatman. To the north and west of the chain lay Florida Bay, laced with sandbars and shoal waters. To the south and east the Florida Reef, the largest coral reef in America, threatened to rip open the hull of any boat that strayed onto its razor-edged rocks. Beyond the reef, the swift, deep waters of the Gulf Stream flowed north through the Straits of Florida. Guy must have regretted having to turn back, to trade the mysterious world of the Florida Keys for the ordered life at his home on Lake Worth.

Waving good-bye to his pals, Charlie began the task of piloting the sloop down through the Keys.[1] He rarely saw a living soul. Few people made any effort to live in the rocky islands, most of them woefully short of drinking water or topsoil.

On their way to Key West, Chevelier's crew went ashore on many of the islands, killing whatever birds they could find. The Frenchman seldom skinned them the same day they were killed. He contended that a wait of one day prevented the birds' blood from ruining the feathers.

One night a squall blew one of the old man's shoes overboard. The next morning they found his shoe near the stern of the *Bonton,* easily visible through the clear Keys water.

As they approached Looe Key, one of the biggest of the Middle Keys, they saw a house where they hoped to find drinking water. Unfortunately the house was locked and boarded up. Charlie climbed to the cistern on the roof where rainwater, the principal source of Keys water, was captured. He lowered a pail of water down to William. From his perch he could look out toward the straits and see the remains of a steamship, long ago wrecked on the reef.

The following day they passed a sharpie, only the second boat they had seen since leaving Biscayne Bay seventeen days earlier. And the day after that, they found an occupied house as they sailed between Little Pine and Big Pine Keys and rounded the north end of Torch Key. When they asked if they could have water, they received a bizarre reply from the man living there:

"Yes, but it is full of apes."

"Come on, boys, let's see what these apes look like," said Charlie. The apes turned out to be large green bullfrogs.

Closer to Key West, they passed eight sloops outward bound from the Island City. All were sailing to the larger Keys and to the mainland to harvest buttonwood and mangrove trees. These would be converted into charcoal for Key West stoves.[2]

About four in the afternoon the *Bonton* arrived at Key West and anchored off John Lowe's dock. It must have been a remarkable experience for Charlie and Henry. Before their youthful eyes unfolded a rare sight for South Florida—a city. Henry had spent all his seventeen years living near the Miami River. He had never seen a city. Charlie, who had moved to Florida from Illinois, had not seen one since he was seven.

Key West in 1885 was well on its way to becoming Florida's largest city, a goal it would reach in 1890 with a census report of more than 18,940.[3] Its docks were filled with the boats of commercial fishermen, and the waterfront air was saturated with the smell of sponges brought back to port from the waters nearby by enterprising divers. "Sponger money" flowed freely in Key West saloons.

In town the boys found city streets lined with wooden buildings—stores, hotels, cafes, and private homes. Even then Key West was a unique place. The southernmost city in the United States, it was not of the South and in a sense not of the United States either. Key West just missed, by thirty miles, the right to claim officially the designation "tropical." A quirk of geography, nothing more. Key West was essentially a Caribbean island, clearly a port of the tropics, flavored with the customs, cultures, and genes of peoples from many islands.

The city's biggest industry, the manufacture of cigars, had brought Cubans skilled in wrapping the tobacco leaves into a "smoke" that delighted Americans after a fine dinner. In Key West the sounds of Spanish filled the air and the smells of Cuban cooking tantalized the boys as they walked along unfamiliar streets.

While Chevelier attended to business matters in town, the boys explored Key West. That night Charlie, a music lover like Guy and Lou Bradley, and the two Wagner boys were delighted by the sweet sounds of a local band playing. One evening they went to a Key West restaurant. "Ordered a steak, tough Florida-round," wrote Charlie. "It sure tasted good to me as it was the first fresh beef I had tasted in a year. After washing this down with a bottle of lemon pop we returned to the boat. On our way back we heard a Cuban serenade that sounded good to me."

On Sunday morning the Wagners, who were Catholics, went to church at St. Mary's Star of the Sea. They told Charlie about the "fine music" they heard there and about the big pipe organ. Late in the afternoon Chevelier came aboard and said he would watch the sloop so Charlie could hear the music at the church.

"The music was sure fine, the best singing I had ever heard although it was in Latin and of course we could not understand a word, but it was fine just the same," wrote Charlie. "And the organ was great . . . on the deep bass notes, the old church would shiver from top to bottom."

Dazzled by life in the big city, Charlie wrote too about a feast given them by the Frenchman: "He gave us two bottles of ginger pop each, and two watermelons, also cake, pie and fresh beef stew for dinner. Right after supper William went up town and got a fifteen-cent package of ice cream for each of us, which was at once put down on the already overloaded stomachs. Results—about 11 o'clock that night all that William and I had swallowed came back and was given to the little fishes. We were sure bad sick the rest of the night."

Fifty years before the *Bonton* arrived, a famous painter visited Key West. He made the island his base of operations as he explored the Keys searching for subjects to paint. His primary interest was bird life, and his name was John James Audubon. Like many who found their way to Key West, he came from the Caribbean. He was born in 1785 in the island nation known today as Haiti.

Audubon arrived in Key West on May 7, 1832, aboard the revenue cutter *Marion*.[4] The first of his series of books *The Birds of America* had already appeared, bringing with it fame, money, and influence. He carried with him letters from the Secretaries of the Navy and the Treasury, directing the captains of naval vessels and revenue cutters to transport him around the islands in search of birds.

The painter, who would later give his name to a great environmental organization, killed birds relentlessly in the Keys. A skilled marksman, he shot some of them to serve as "models" for his paintings. He preferred to draw freshly killed birds rather than work from mounted specimens or bird skins as earlier painters did. Many of the birds he killed, however, were victims of his reckless gunfire into massed groups of pelicans and cormorants. He was also known to shoot birds from the decks of ships, purely for sport. Out of the Keys came some of his most magnificent bird paintings.

As a naturalist, Chevelier would have been familiar with Audubon's work. Neither found anything objectionable in shooting birds. Audubon would have found it inconceivable that a sky so full of birds could ever yield to the desolation the plume hunters would someday bring. Chevelier saw it happening, but few hunters in 1885 were willing to stanch the bloody flow of money from the feather trade.

When the sloop was properly stocked again, Chevelier and crew set out for what would be the major part of their hunt. They first sailed out across Florida Bay to Oyster Keys, just south of Cape Sable.

"We could see birds on these keys, so we anchored and went after them," Charlie wrote. "Henry killed a pelican and I killed one. We returned to the *Bonton* to wait for sunset as the birds are not nesting on these islands. Near dark a big lot of egrets, white herons, Louisiana herons and curlew came to sleep on the Key. We went after them. William killed one egret. Henry killed five, and I killed twelve and one white heron."

The *Bonton* cruised next to a horseshoe-shaped island called Sandy Key. Two herons and a clapper rail were all they killed, far less than Audubon had shot when he visited the island in 1832. They anchored that night just off Cape Sable, near the James A. Waddell coconut grove.[5]

Mosquitoes were so fierce that Charlie made the rash claim "They cannot get any thicker." He found he was wrong the next night, even though he anchored the *Bonton* a mile and a half from land in about six feet of water.

"Dead calm all night, and this morning," he wrote sadly. "When we got out from under our mosquito bars there was not a spot as large as a pin head on that boat from the water line to the tip of the mast that did not have a mosquito on it. We fought them for about two hours before we could stop to make coffee."

In between their two mosquito battles Henry, the youngest of the crew, underwent a strange experience, one that reveals the desolation of the Cape Sable country. Just beyond the cape's northwestern point they found what they thought at first was the mouth of a channel leading from the Gulf of Mexico into Whitewater Bay, a large body of water at the southernmost end of the Everglades. The channel turned out to be not the entrance to Whitewater Bay but rather the ominously named Shark River, narrow and deep and lined with thick mangroves towering sixty feet above the river like skyscrapers, creating the illusion of a dark and mysterious canyon. The sharks that filled the waters added to the sense of foreboding.

"The tide was with us and soon the channel took the form and appearance of a good sized river," wrote Charlie. "Having wind and tide with us, we kept going we did not know where. The place looked wild and lonely.

"About three o'clock it seemed to get on Henry's nerves. And we saw that he was crying, he would not tell us why. He was just plain scared."

At about this time the tide turned. The Frenchman deemed it best to take the tide back to the Gulf and "relieve the feelings" of young Henry.

After a large kill of brown pelicans, they sailed on up the coast to Panther Key. There they found an old palmetto shack inhabited by a friend of the Frenchman, "an old Portuguese named Gomez with his old cracker wife."

For a hermit, Juan Gomez had become a remarkably famous character.[6] A teller of tall tales, he charmed the correspondents of George Grinnell's *Forest and Stream*. They dropped by often, knowing they could always count on a good story. Gomez claimed he was born in 1778, which would have made him more than a hundred years old when the *Bonton* arrived. He said he had served with Napoleon and had been a cabin boy for a pirate named Jose Gaspar, sometimes called Gasparilla. Some of his best stories were about his pirating days with Gasparilla, who probably never existed.

Gomez claimed he had fought in the Battle of Okeechobee in the Second Seminole War on Christmas Day 1837 in the army of Colonel Zachary Taylor, destined to become America's twelfth president. He could also spin yarns about his days as a slaver and later as a blockade runner during the Civil War. Gomez's two-room palmetto shack had been built by two plume buyers named Pinicker and Brown and later given to him. He was probably one of their many suppliers.

The old pirate piloted the crew up a creek in search of birds, but they found nothing but a few roseate spoonbills too far away to shoot. Late in the afternoon they dropped Gomez off at his place on Panther Key and sailed on to the big island called Marco. There they met Captain Bill Collier, who served them a supper of cabbage and eggplant.

"I can tell you it tasted good to us," Charlie reported. "We have been living mostly on hard bread and coffee for the past four weeks."

Captain Collier's hospitality was in sharp contrast with the reception the crew generally found on the west coast. Most people, Charlie claimed, viewed them with suspicion.

At Estero Bay they saw a sloop hard aground on the inside beach, evidently placed there to permit the captain, an old Italian, to clean the bottom at low tide. A Cracker boy of about ten worked with him as cook and helper. When the boy turned the coffeepot over, the old man screamed at him, "Jackassfoolmonkeybaboon, donn you know better than that?" Thereafter, they always referred to the old Italian as Monkeybaboon. The sloop he was preparing to clean was the *Rona Jenkins*. Years earlier Charlie had seen the boat when it was being built by Wash Jenkins at the Fort Lauderdale House of Refuge.

On small islands north of Estero Bay they found a large nesting place and killed forty-three pelicans. After they returned to the *Bonton*, a man named Frank Johnson came up to their boat and told them he had seen them shooting birds. He told them he had heard of a law against shooting them in their nests. He thought they had better stop. Charlie told them they had just come from the county seat in faraway Key West, where Chevelier had looked into the matter and concluded there was no law against shooting the birds.

The next day, just to make sure, Chevelier went into Punta Rassa, a small settlement consisting mostly of the Tarpon House, a famed sporting inn that drew fishermen from as far away as Great Britain, and a large wharf used for loading cattle onto vessels bound for Havana. The Frenchman wanted to find out if there were any changes in the law, and also to see if he had any mail. Chevelier was well known in the area. While in Punta Rassa, he probably checked in with the local telegrapher J. W. Atkins, an amateur ornithologist of note who would have known about any new developments involving birds.

"We found that there was not any law against shooting birds in the rookeries or anywhere else," Charlie wrote. "That cracker, Frank Johnson, wanted to turn us off so he could have the birds for himself."

Within a couple of days a mail carrier in a small boat directed them to a rookery near Charlotte Harbor. They found thousands of curlew, cormorants, Louisiana herons, reddish egrets, white egrets, and a number of other species. The air was so full of birds they could not see through them. Since they did not want to kill the curlew, they struggled to pick out the plume birds in the bewildering mass overhead.

The Frenchman, still hampered by his hand injury, just sat there pointing his gun first one way and then another, not firing a shot. After about five minutes he gave up. "Mine God, 'tis too much birds in this contrie. I can not shoot."

Before they left the rookery, they killed nineteen reddish egrets, two night herons, three Louisiana herons, six white herons, and one American egret. They also gathered 104 curlew eggs.

By now the trip was winding down. Charlie wrote: "As the plume birds are about gone there is not enough to pay us to stay here longer. . . . I do not think we will come back as all are getting tired of the trip and want to start for home."

And finally, from the Old Frenchman himself: "Everybody commence very tired this time, the best we go back to Miami."

As they sailed back, they visited again with Monkeybaboon, who gave them water and a short talk on religion: "God is like the wind, you can feel it, you know it is there, yet you cannot see it. It is the same with God. You can feel Him and you know He is there, yet you cannot see Him."

Squalls bothered them throughout their return to Biscayne Bay. Finally in August they sailed up the Miami River to Wagner's place, the voyage at long last over. The total recorded kill for the cruise, plus the two side trips by Charlie and the Bradley boys, amounted to 1,397 individual birds of thirty-six species.

The Frenchman was well pleased. "The Bongton the best ah boat in Florida."

5 The Barefoot Mailman

IN THE SUMMER OF 1885, not long after the Bradley boys returned from their adventure with the Old Frenchman, the United States Post Office reentered the lives of the Bradley family. Mail delivery between the growing pioneer settlements on Lake Worth and those on Biscayne Bay proved a slow and cumbersome task. Using official U.S. Post Office channels, a letter from the Hypoluxo-Lantana area to Miami, just sixty-six miles to the south, could take six weeks to two months. The letter went first by boat and stagecoach to the lighthouse community of Jupiter, twenty-two miles to the north. From there the letter traveled by Indian River steamboat to the railhead at Titusville and then by train to New York City, where it was placed aboard a steamer to Havana. From Cuba the letter would be transported aboard a trading schooner to Miami.[1]

The Post Office came up with a plan to cut the delivery time to three days. During the Civil War a mailman named Long John Holman had carried the mail from Fort Dallas on the Miami River to St. Augustine by walking along the beach, thus avoiding hostile Indians, wild animals, and Florida's dense jungle growth. Long John even found a cave to hide in among coral rocks along the beach near today's posh Gold Coast town of Gulf Stream.[2] Why not try the beach highway again for the growing settlements on the southeast coast?

Edwin R. Bradley, whose father had contributed significantly to the operations of the Chicago post office, entered a bid and won the contract for the barefoot route. The job called for one round-trip a week, from Lake Worth to Biscayne Bay and back, for an annual wage of six hundred dollars. It would be a physically demanding task for E. R., now a man of forty-five, but he could count on his elder son, Lou, to alternate with him in walking the route.

Lou was assigned to work out the logistics of the barefoot route. Under his plan the mailman would go by boat over to a growing settlement that would soon assume the name Palm Beach, pick up the mail, then row to the south end of Lake Worth. Here the serious walking would begin. The mailman would take off his shoes and walk on the sandy beach to the Orange Grove House of Refuge, where he would spend the night. The next morning he would walk to the Hillsboro Inlet, then row across in a boat which he would conceal in the mangroves on the south side so it would be available for him on his return route. That night either Lou or his father would with sadness in his heart sleep at the Fort Lauderdale House of Refuge, near the grave of little Flora Bradley. In the morning the mailman would cross New River Inlet before walking another ten miles to Baker's Haulover at the head of Biscayne Bay. From there he would use a small boat fitted with oars and a sail for a twelve-mile trip to the Miami post office. After spending the night in Miami, the mailman would load up his mailbag for the return trip, a route of 136 miles—56 miles by sailboat or rowboat and 80 miles along the beach on foot. The carrier was always back home by late Saturday, leaving him free on Sunday to work in the family vegetable garden.

The barefoot mailman, as he came to be called years later,[3] carried his shoes over his shoulder and learned quickly that the best place for walking was the area where the surf washes the sand. This was the firmest part of the beach. Naturally the carrier rolled his trousers up to guard against the occasional bigger wave. The barefoot mailmen developed a special way of walking, since the slant of the beach made for a tiring trip. Walking south, the mailman made his stride on the right leg on the higher part of the beach quicker than the left and reversed the process when going back north. This kept the legs and feet in excellent, and balanced, condition and lessened the chance of excessive fatigue. A person who mastered this technique was called a good beach walkist.

The mail pouches used by the mailman were custom-built for the barefoot route. Regular letter pouches at that time were made of heavy cowhide. Pouches for the beach route were made of lightweight canvas, about fifteen inches wide and thirty inches long. Most of the time this pouch could be rolled into a small bundle and carried in a haversack slung on a strap over the shoulder. One later carrier who speared a number of fish trapped in a tidal pool carried those he couldn't eat in the pouch. Complaints from Miami about the smell of the letters put an immediate stop to this practice.

E. R. Bradley preferred to walk the beach by night. Why? To avoid Indians, he would explain, displaying a penchant for self-dramatization that he would pass on to his younger son, Guy. Actually, in 1885 Indians presented no problem, and large land animals such as bear and panther were seen less and less as new settlers were seen more and more. The lengthy walk made it a strenuous job, too strenuous for fifteen-year-old Guy, but not really a dangerous one—at least as long as the boats at the inlets were in the right location for the mailman. Without a boat the inlets could be deadly. Tidal currents could be strong, and the waters were often patrolled by sharks or alligators.

For more than a year E. R. and Lou walked the barefoot route, a tiring and eventually boring routine. Occasionally, however, the outside world intruded, and never with more gleeful impact than during the happy autumn days of 1886 following a shipwreck that would pass into legend as the Great Wine Wreck.

One glorious morning Charlie Pierce heard a rapid knocking on his door. On the front porch stood his close friend George Charter, highly excited.

"The beach is covered with wine casks, hundreds of them," George said.

Charlie had seen the beach covered with seaweed, and sometimes Portuguese men-o'-war with their painful stinging tentacles. Never had he seen a beach covered with wine casks.

"What a sight met our gaze when we came out on the shore," Charlie later wrote. "One-hundred gallon casks of Spanish claret lay strewn along the coast, so close together one could have walked for a mile along this part of the beach without once having to step off a cask."

The Bradleys quickly joined the wine salvagers. Some of the casks were still floating in the water. The wine brigade rolled the casks onto the beach and then on to their homes or their boats. Hannibal Pierce, Charlie's father, launched an immediate search for bottles and jugs, fearful that South Florida's voracious weevil population would bore holes in the wooden casks. The Pierces managed to bottle a hundred gallons of Spanish claret. They also salvaged three or four fifteen-gallon kegs of Malaga and another wine that was branded Double Superior. Like a latter-day wine taster, Charlie pronounced it "very sweet and mild, but very strong in alcohol."

Whence came these vineyard glories? The pioneer settlers along the coast knew the wine was of Spanish origin because of the brand names on the heads of the casks. But there was no flotsam ashore other than the casks, and no one had heard of any wrecks along the coast. Whatever the name of the ship was, its cargo must have been a large one. Wine casks in quantity were found on the beaches from Palm Beach to the Keys. Some were carried to homes and stored or rebottled; some were buried in the sand; some, unfortunately, floated back out to sea. Jack Peacock, keeper of the Fort Lauderdale House of Refuge, bathed in the wine, hopeful it might cure his arthritis. Indians boated down the New River and tried to tow casks back to their camps in the Everglades. Inside a week all the casks had disappeared from the beaches. But what a week! A mammoth binge followed by a mammoth hangover.

E. R. Bradley came up with an inspired plan for his share of the wine. He buried casks along the barefoot route at such exotic locations as Seven-Mile Tripod. On his appointed rounds he could pause for a drink as he made his way along the beach. Fresh water was fairly hard to find; wine, after the wreck, considerably less so.

In the early summer of 1887 E. R. Bradley gave up the barefoot route. The Bradleys had operated the speeded-up postal service for close to two years without any undue complications, but at best the job was a restricting, demanding one. And Bradley was a restless man. In giving up the route he proved also to be lucky, very lucky.

The mail route relinquished by Bradley was taken over by George Charter and Ed Hamilton. Ed had come to Hypoluxo from Trigg County, a small rural county in western Kentucky.

The fall of 1887 was extremely stormy, even by South Florida standards. No hurricanes struck that year, but squalls and gales pounded the coast and drenched the tiny settlements with torrential rains. Rivers—the Hillsboro, the New, the Miami—flooded all along the coast.

Because it was his turn, Hamilton reported to the Pierces' on Hypoluxo Island on Sunday, October 9, 1887.[4] Hannibal Pierce was postmaster and Charlie his chief assistant. At the noonday dinner at the Pierces,' Hamilton complained of not feeling well.

"Why don't you spend the night here?" suggested Charlie. "Louie can make the trip with you tomorrow."

Ed shook his head and told them he carried his own "medicine chest," a bottle of Perry Davis Pain-killer and a spoon. For a man of his strength and conditioning, he insisted, the walk that afternoon to the Orange Grove House of Refuge should be easy enough.

Hamilton had no particular difficulty in reaching the lifesaving station. He chatted awhile with his friend, keeper Steve Andrews, and then turned in for a night's sleep. In the morning Mrs. Andrews gave Ed a good breakfast and sent him on his way toward New River and his next overnight stop, the Fort Lauderdale House of Refuge. On his head was a wide-brimmed hat, on his back a black oilcloth knapsack containing food, water, and utensils, plus the locked mail sack and his portable "medicine chest."

A half day's walk south from the Orange Grove station lay the inlet. There the waters of the Hillsboro River roared through on their journey from the rain-drenched Everglades to the sea. Hamilton should have reached the Hillsboro Inlet by noon on Monday and should have been back to Hypoluxo by roughly noon on Saturday. But Ed Hamilton did not return on Saturday. As the afternoon wore on, Charlie became uneasy, recalling that the mailman had left the Pierces' home in less than tip-top shape. The next morning Charlie sailed over to the beach to wait for Ed. He could look to the south and see the mailman when he appeared on the beach. But Ed never came.

Charlie, who had to visit Palm Beach on business, notified George Charter. Ed's partner was so upset he formed a search party. When Charlie returned from Palm Beach on Wednesday, Charter gave him the news.

Charter and another carrier had gone to the Orange Grove station and spent the night with Andrews. After supper, as they sat in the living room reviewing over and over again the meager scraps of information on Hamilton, they heard from the beach a faint call—a man's voice. Could it be Ed?

They rushed out of the house. All they could see was the dark form of a boat at the water's edge, and a man struggling to pull the boat up on the beach, out of the reach of the waves. They ran to the boat, calling to Ed.

But it wasn't Ed. The man in the darkness was Charles Coman, keeper of the Fort Lauderdale House of Refuge. He too was looking for Hamilton. Hamilton had never reached Coman's station. He should have arrived at the refuge on Tuesday. When he failed to appear, Coman became uneasy, and with good reason.

On Monday, the day Hamilton was due at Fort Lauderdale, a stranger had appeared, walking down the beach from the north. Coman asked him how he had crossed the swollen Hillsboro Inlet. The man told him a party of hunters with a portable boat had carried him across the inlet. Coman did not believe the story. He believed the man had used Ed's boat, leaving the mailman no way to cross the inlet except to try to swim. When Hamilton failed to arrive on time at the station, Coman set out to investigate. Finding no trace of Ed at the south side of the inlet, he continued up to the Orange Grove house.

At daylight the next morning Charter and Coman set out from Orange Grove, walking down the beach along the route Ed would have taken. When they reached the inlet, they headed straight to the place where the mailman hid his boat.

They found no boat. What they found was Ed's knapsack hanging on a limb of a sea grape tree. In the bag they found the mail pouch, his trousers, and his shirt. They found, too, his spoon and a bottle of Perry Davis Painkiller. Near the water lay his underclothes. The only conclusion they could reach was that Ed had taken off his underwear just prior to entering the water to try unsuccessfully to swim the inlet.

"Hamilton's gone," George told Charlie on his return. "The sharks got him. Sharks ate him. He tried to swim the inlet and sharks got him."

The little settlement at Hypoluxo was stunned by the news. Hamilton was a popular man—"a grand Christian man," Charlie's little sister Lillie called him.

Charlie and Louie were convinced one more search should be made. They set sail in the *Ibis* and arrived at the Hillsboro Inlet at midafternoon. They made camp on the south point near where the mailman usually kept his boat. Charlie and Louie knew the area well from their explorations on the first leg of the cruise of the *Bonton*. They searched up the river, along the beach, and at an inlet swarming with alligators washed down from the Glades. No trace was ever found of Ed. Charlie Pierce's conclusion was that alligators, not sharks, had killed Ed Hamilton.

The government continued the barefoot route until late 1892 when a rock road was completed from Lantana to the Miami area. After that the Bay Biscayne Stage Line took over mail delivery, and the barefoot mailman became a Florida legend.

$\mathcal{O}$ Tycoons of the Plume Trade

WILLIAM EARL DODGE SCOTT was an unlikely candidate for a career as a wilderness ornithologist. A native of Brooklyn, New York, educated at Cornell and Harvard, and eventually curator of the Department of Ornithology at the College of New Jersey (later Princeton University), Scott had been crippled by a serious illness at the age of five. But he shrugged off his handicaps and, with the aid of crutches and a cane, hobbled into remote areas of Florida and the Caribbean to see for himself the condition of wildlife in the warm climates. He emerged as one of the most perceptive observers of the horrors of the plume trade.

Scott wrote a series of articles about plume birds, plume hunters, and plume traders in the Gulf Coast rookeries, which were published in 1887 in *The Auk,* the scholarly journal of the American Ornithologists' Union.[1] Since he had visited Florida's Ten Thousand Islands as early as 1875, Scott had benchmarks for comparison when he returned in 1886. In just a little over a decade he found a different world, and the change was far from a healthy one.

In his entry for Wednesday, June 2, 1886, he wrote:

About three miles from the extreme end of Point Pinellas, in Boca Ciega Bay, is the group of islands that once formed what is known as Maximo Rookery. This is at least two hundred acres in extent, and is covered with a dense growth of the several kinds of mangrove and forms a point particularly attractive to birds either as a roosting or breeding place. I had been here six years before and it fairly teemed with bird life then. Every tree and bush on this large area contained from two to six or eight nests. A perfect cloud of birds were always to be seen hovering over islands in the spring and early summer months, and conspicuous among them were brown pelicans, man-o'-war birds, reddish egrets, Florida cormorants, Louisiana herons, American egrets, snowy herons, little blue herons, great blue herons, and both kinds of night herons. . . . It was truly a wonderful sight, and I have never seen so many thousands of birds together at any single point.

On the day of his return, he encountered a different sight:

From the water, as we approached, only a few cormorants were to be seen, possibly 75 in all, and though I spent several hours looking over the various parts of the island I found no other large birds breeding, absolutely not a single pair of herons of any kind; five or six Louisiana herons feeding on a small sand flat at one of the extremities of the island were all the herons observed in the vicinity.

When I previously visited this point, A. Lechevallier had located on the mainland about three quarters of a mile away; here he had built a house and was killing birds on the island for the feather market. He or his assistants had then been there a little over a year, and I am told . . . that it took these men five breeding seasons to break up, by killing and frightening the birds away, this once incomparable breeding resort. . . . He regarded this as his particular preserve, and went so far as to order outsiders, who came to kill herons and other birds, off his ground. The rookery being destroyed he had now given up his residence here.[2]

Scott became a familiar figure on Florida's west coast. He appeared at bays, waterways, islands, and rookeries, equipped with cane and crutches and the tools of a professional ornithologist. A child of his times, Scott was not one who shrank from killing birds. He was a scientific collector, accustomed to shooting and skinning birds and, as a highly skilled taxidermist, preparing them for eventual use in the museum at Princeton.

Even with his crippled leg, Scott amazed people with his mobility on land or water. He called himself a "fairly good swimmer." One old Cracker even called him web-footed like "Mr. Debil." He was a tough man, capable of exploring mountain and jungle regions and waters that others considered dangerous. But tough as he was, he had no stomach for the slaughter he saw on his five-month collecting stint along the Gulf Coast.

The boat chartered for the trip was a small sloop, the *Tantalus,* prophetically named after the Greek king for whom the gods prescribed an unusual punishment. Whatever he reached for receded from his grasp, just as the plume birds were drifting away from Scott.

The first jolt was not long in coming. The *Tantalus,* skippered by a Captain Baker, sailed out the Anclote River from Tarpon Springs to the Anclote Keys, just three miles out in the Gulf of Mexico. Six years earlier Scott had seen "a perfect cloud of birds" above the islands. Now the keys were deserted.

He found the same story when he reached Charlotte Harbor, a large saltwater bay already earning fame as a paradise for the sports fishermen seeking tarpon, the Silver King. It was ringed with small mangrove islands. Captain Baker, an old sponger and fisherman who had sailed the area for more than a quarter of a century, showed Scott an island of about sixty acres.

"I've seen that island so covered with white curlew that it looked from a distance like a big white sheet had been thrown over the mangroves," he told Scott.

And what did they see this time? Two herons during the cruise of some forty miles.

At a settlement called Hickory Bluff at the mouth of Peas Creek,[3] Scott talked to the postmaster. Birds had been plentiful, Scott was told, but for the past two years they "had been so persecuted, for their plumes for the Northern market that they were practically exterminated, or at least driven away from all their old haunts." The postmaster talked at length about the plume trade.

"I further learned," wrote Scott, "that all of the gunners and hunters in the country round had up to this year reaped a very considerable income from this source. Birds were killed, and the plumes taken from the backs, head and breast and the carcass thrown to the buzzards."

The market for the plume trade was just a short distance down the coast at the town of Fort Myers. It was a cowtown that boasted a number of ships and businesses, a weekly newspaper, and a resident population of roughly 350 people. Its most illustrious winter resident was an inventor named Tom Edison. He maintained a big house and laboratory on a beautifully landscaped estate on the Caloosahatchee River.[4]

The wide Caloosahatchee was navigable by steamboat all the way back to Lake Okeechobee, with a boost from one short canal. This made Fort Myers the central market for plumes from the lake, the western Everglades, and the Ten Thousand Islands. During the winter, the postmaster told Scott, more plume buyers came down from the north, many of them calling themselves taxidermists. They equipped the local hunters with the latest breechloaders and ammunition.

One man, Scott was told, had been coming down to the west coast for the past four years. This hunter employed between forty and sixty gunners, furnishing them with all necessary supplies and then buying plumes and flat skins from his hunters. The prices ranged from twenty cents to two dollars and a half for a skin, the average being about forty cents apiece. The man, the postmaster said, was "down south now." Scott decided he had better be on the lookout for this most enterprising of all the hunters.

Near Hickory Bluff, Scott sought out rookeries where he was told birds could still be found in large numbers. At the mouth of the Myakka River, which flowed into Charlotte Harbor, he found only a deserted rookery. Farther upstream he encountered better luck, finding a small mangrove island inhabited by several species of herons and egrets.

"Up to the present time, though I had been away on a trip for a week," he wrote, "not a single bird had been collected. So, after dinner I went to the neighborhood of the rookery, where about two hundred birds in all were congregated, and in the course of the afternoon I took some twenty birds of the several kinds—a pair or so of each. The rookery had evidently often been disturbed before, and the birds were very shy and only to be taken at long range, flying."

Like other collectors of his time, Scott had no trouble in drawing a distinction between killing twenty of the two hundred birds in a rookery for scientific purposes and killing all two hundred for a bigger payoff. After his day at the rookery, Scott spent most of the next morning transforming the birds he had killed into properly preserved skins.

While aboard the anchored *Tantalus,* he was visited on two separate occasions by hunters trying to sell him egret plumes. "They seemed much surprised to find that I did not wish to buy the material in question," he wrote, "and told me I was the only birdman they had met who was not eager to obtain plumes."

Scott made notes on the prices the men were asking:

American egret, 40 cents (the only part of the bird used being the long feathers of the back); the snowy egret, 55 cents (in addition to the back plumes those of the throat or breast and head are utilized); reddish egret, 40 cents (simply the back plumes); Louisiana heron, 10–15 cents (only the plumes of the back are utilized); Ward's heron, 75 cents to one dollar (plumes of breast and back); and roseate spoonbill, $2 to $5 (flat skin). A flat skin is the bird skin split underneath from the bill to vent and skinned so that the whole is perfectly flat when dry. Generally, the legs are cut off, and sometimes the wings, and even the head.

Both men told Scott even more about the man who employed vast numbers of gunners. Particularly helpful to him was Abe Wilkerson. Abe was on his way up the Myakka River to lakes in the interior where he hoped to find large rookeries of snowy egrets, the best-paying species.

"I've made many a dollar from plumes," said Wilkerson. "I use a .22-calibre Winchester rifle."

With a .22 he could hide away in a rookery and "by using the lightest kind of cartridge get many more birds than with a shotgun." The report, he told Scott, was hardly greater than the snapping of a branch and was scarcely noticed by the birds. In this way he had been able to kill more than four hundred plume birds in less than four days in a large rookery down south.

Scott proceeded down through Matlacha Pass between the mainland and Pine Island, the largest of the many islands in the Charlotte Harbor area. He was seeking an island that Wilkerson described as a breeding place for reddish egrets. In the late afternoon, he wrote, he found it.

> The trees were full of nests, some of which still contained eggs, and hundreds of broken eggs strewed the ground everywhere. Fish crows and both kinds of buzzards were present in great numbers and were rapidly destroying the remaining eggs. I found a huge pile of dead, half-decayed birds, lying on the ground which had apparently been killed for a day or two. All of them had the "plumes" taken off with a patch of skin from the back, and some had the wings off. I counted over 200 birds treated this way. The most common species was the reddish egret, though there were about as many Louisiana herons; the other species were the snowy heron, the great white egret, and the little blue heron in both phases of plumage. There were also a few pelicans, white ibises, and one or two great blue herons. I remained there till almost dark, but did not

fire at any of the few frightened herons (about 50 in all) which came to roost on the island. Among these I noticed a few reddish egrets and two of the so-called Peale's egrets, but most of the birds were the commoner species of heron. This was the rookery that Mr. Wilkerson had spoken of; within the last few days it had been almost destroyed, hundreds of old birds having been killed and thousands of eggs broken.

I do not know of a more horrible and brutal exhibition of wanton destruction than that which I witnessed here.

The following morning a saddened Scott and Captain Baker explored the nearby islands. Ten years before, the whole region had teemed with bird life. Now only a handful remained. Farther south they found a few birds, apparently those driven from the large rookery they saw the evening before.

All of them were very shy and suspicious, being startled by the slightest noise or movement, and none of the birds would come near the island until the small boat had returned to the sloop. I learned later that the birds on the island had been much persecuted by gunners.

Captain Baker anchored off the cattle port of Punta Rassa near the mouth of the Caloosahatchee. There Scott encountered Frank Johnson, a professional hunter.

"What do you hunt?" asked Scott.

"Almost anything that wears feathers," Johnson said. His primary targets were the snowy heron, American egret, and reddish egret. These, he said, brought the highest prices when sold to "taxidermists," as the plume buyers preferred to be called.

"I wish there was some law to protect the birds," said Johnson, "at least during the breeding time, which wouldn't be broken. But since everybody else is pluming, I made up my mind I might as well have my share."

And who was the "taxidermist" Johnson sold his plumes to?

Mr. J. H. Batty, of New York City.[5]

And what was he buying?

"Almost anything that wears feathers, but more particularly the herons, spoonbills, and snowy birds," said Johnson.

Pressing Johnson for more details, Scott learned that Batty was the man who employed gunners all along the Gulf Coast, from the Cedar Keys to Key West. Batty, it seemed, had made regular trips to the region for the past three winters. He traveled along the coast in a small schooner, supplying Cracker gunners with breech-loading shotguns and ammunition. Johnson had brought one of Batty's guns and was using it when Scott met him. One barrel was for .12-gauge shot, the other was a small-bore rifle. Johnson used the rifle barrel for pelicans and, because it was quiet, for shooting the smaller herons at close range in the rookeries.

Johnson told Scott of the ease with which a gunner could find thousands of birds in the rookeries five or six years earlier. Now, he said, absolutely none remained.

The year before, about eighty to a hundred brown pelicans had selected a small mangrove island near his home for nesting. They hatched out their young under the protection of Johnson, who planned to let them rear their young birds. One afternoon when Johnson was away, a hunter came in by boat and killed off all the older birds, close to a hundred in number, while they were feeding their young. Several hundred young birds, about three weeks old, remained, too young to care for themselves. They were simply left there to starve to death in their nests, or to be eaten by raccoons and buzzards.

The hunter who killed the birds had come into the area aboard the *Bonton.* His name was Jean Chevelier.

Johnson's tales about the slaughter of birds must have convinced Scott that Wednesday, May 12, was the day to make at least one small gesture of protest against the activities of Batty and Chevelier. That day, at a rookery they visited, he paid Johnson two dollars not to shoot any birds.

At Punta Rassa, Scott met J. W. Atkins, the assistant telegraph operator for the Western Union Telegraph Company—an important post, since the telegraph stretched from Punta Rassa to Key West and then on to Havana. Atkins was an enthusiastic and informed collector of birds and, like Scott, a contributor to *The Auk.* Ironically, Atkins's boss was the ebullient George Shultz, hotelier, restaurateur, and buyer of plumes.

While waiting for his mail at Punta Rassa, Scott ran into Wilkerson again. His trip to Myakka Lake had not been fruitful. Persistent hunting had made the birds so shy that he had obtained only seventy-five plumes on a lengthy hunt. Scott hired Wilkerson to make the trip back to Tarpon Springs with him.

As they sailed past the Boca Grande rookery in Charlotte Harbor, they heard the constant discharge of guns on an island where roseate spoonbills lived. "Almost a war of extermination," Scott called it. The birds, he observed, had become disoriented in their nesting habits from too much persecution by relentless gunners.

About four o'clock the afternoon of May 24, a schooner, forty-five feet in length, came from the direction of Big Gasparilla Pass, named for Juan Gomez's mythical pirate king, and anchored within two hundred feet of the *Tantalus*. Four crewmen from the sharpie went ashore "and from the time they landed until dark there was a perfect fusillade." Scott found they were killing all kinds of shorebirds and least terns.

"Whose boat is it?" he asked.

"Mr. Batty's," he was told.

Scott learned further that Batty was down on the beach shooting and would be back for supper. The men who told Scott they were collecting for the plume market had bunches of Wilson's plover, least terns, and various kinds of sandpipers. The skins were removed from the birds, partly filled with cotton, wrapped in paper, and packed away to be finished in New York. Batty's men were killing and preparing between 100 and 150 birds a day.

That night Scott called on the mastermind behind the hunters.

Batty, now in his early forties, was born in Springfield, Massachusetts. He showed a great fondness for natural history early in life. Before he was out of his teens, he was collecting birds and mammals in the mountains of Colorado for the Hayden Survey. The trip to the Rockies must have impressed him. When he opened a taxidermy business in New Utrecht, New York, he used as his logo the head of a Rocky Mountain sheep. His ad, appearing regularly in *Forest and Stream,* called him a "Dealer in objects of Natural History, Dining Room Taxidermy, Game Birds on Shields and Stands, Backs, Heads, Antlers, Carved Heads. Taxidermist Supplies, Skins and eggs for collections, aquaria and stock, Insects, Chrysalides, Coral, Shells, etc."

There was little in the natural history line that Batty had missed in his busy life, leading *The Auk* to write years later that he "was probably more familiar with a larger portion of the wilds of tropical America than any other traveler or explorer."

Despite Scott's growing uneasiness with the Gulf Coast bird slaughter, he and Batty seem to have hit it off rather well. Batty talked openly with him. And why not? Both were interested in scientific collection, and the plume trade was still a good many years away from being illegal. To Batty, the business was the source of a large income that also permitted him to leave New York during the cold months and live and work in the outdoors in Florida's balmy weather.

Scott apparently was less than overcome by revulsion at Batty's activities. The next morning he went to the beach and shot birds with Batty, "knots, black-bellied sandpipers sanderlings and turnstones over decoys, all these species being used by Mr. Batty in his feather business."

At the same time, two other members of Batty's gun crew were killing Wilson's plover and least terns. The terns were particularly in demand for the millinery business. Batty paid his gunners ten to fifteen cents each for these birds.

Further, wrote Scott:

> All owls, and particularly the barred owl, are desirable. The feathers of these, as well as of hawks, bleached by processes that Mr. Batty decribed to me are used for hats and other decorations. One of Mr. Batty's employees told me that they had left a party at the pass below, where they were killing the same kinds of birds, and that Mr. Batty was constantly purchasing and trading with native and other gunners for plumes and round and flat skins of all the desirable birds of the region.
>
> Not less than sixty men were working on the Gulf Coast for Batty in this way. From time to time, as we were together, I picked up these facts, and I have been careful to understate rather than overestimate the destruction that was going on from this single source.

As he continued up the coast, Scott found the same story everywhere, rookeries "broken up" by plume hunters near Casey's Pass, Big Sarasota Pass, the Manatee shore on lower Tampa Bay, John's Pass—the list went on and on. When Scott returned to his base of operations at Tarpon Springs, he heard even more reports about Batty. The man was now shooting at a place six miles to the north of Tarpon Springs, a place aptly named Trouble Creek. There he bought all the birds the gunners could kill except for white ibis. He bought hawks, owls, and Florida quail. His prices ranged from ten cents to seventy-five cents, with as much as a dollar for some birds, such as the great blue heron.

Later, back in the peaceful confines of Princeton, Scott summarized his trip in a series of three scholarly papers published in *The Auk*. He concluded:

> It is scarcely necessary to draw any conclusions or inferences. This great and growing evil speaks for itself. I have the name and addresses of some fifty dealers in various towns in Florida and the principal cities of the country. Merchants in New York and other centers are buying every month the skins and plumes of Florida birds. The price paid for such material, notwithstanding the efforts made to create sympathy for the birds, and a feeling against using the feathers for hats and other decorative purposes, is each year becoming higher, showing how great is the demand and how profitable the traffic is to these milliners.

But the tide was turning—slowly, to be sure—against the plume trade. Even Batty, the most successful of all the plume tycoons, would in the 1890s turn his back on a business that had brought him large returns. He was, after all, also a scientist. Once he thought through the frightening results of his handiwork, he left the plume trade.

Others would prove more difficult to convince.

7 Cuthbert's Rookery

SOMEWHERE DOWN NEAR the tip of Florida, hidden deep in the vast mangrove wilderness, lay an island sanctuary where the wading birds—the egrets, herons, ibis, and spoonbills—could nest in peace, safe for a while from the relentless pursuit of the plume hunters. So remote was the island that no white hunter had ever reached it. Still, the plumers knew it was there. They had watched the flights of birds to the south, down through the Ten Thousand Islands and the Everglades. From the Indians they had heard stories about a huge rookery, possibly the last great bird rookery in the eastern part of the country. For the crafty plume hunter who found it, the rookery could mean a small fortune.[1]

In Florida, where the bird population promised the richest rewards for hunters, the plume birds had been demolished first near the populated areas in the northern part of the state. Then as birds and hunters moved farther south, the rookeries around Tampa Bay had been decimated. Virtually wiped out at the same time were the dense bird colonies ringing the shores of the huge inland lake called Okeechobee. From there birds were driven farther south into the Everglades and the Ten Thousand Islands until only the remnants of a once enormous bird population struggled to survive in the impenetrable mangrove wilderness near Cape Sable. By the late 1880s there were no large concentrations of plume birds remaining within easy reach of any of Florida's settled areas.

Only an extended, well-supplied, and well-planned expedition deep into the wilderness held any hope for hunters seeking the rich rewards they had enjoyed in the past. Most were hesitant to venture into the mysterious Cape Sable country. The probability of an expensive failure discouraged most of them. Long distances meant supply problems, for a plume hunter had to carry guns, ammunition, knives to scalp the dead birds, and arsenic to preserve the beauty of the plumes until they could be delivered to the buyers scattered around South Florida's tiny settlements. Maps were unreliable, mangroves were confusing and difficult to penetrate, mosquitoes and horseflies were unbearable. And to make it worse, stories of giant serpents at the cape further fed the fear of the unknown.

From his modest home on Marco Island, owned outright in the 1880s by Captain William Collier, an adventurous hunter named George Elliott Cuthbert decided to seek the rookery of rookeries.[2] He had learned the intricacies of navigating the lower west coast of Florida, including the Cape Sable coastline, while serving as skipper of Collier's schooner, which carried mail and supplies between Fort Myers and South Florida's only real city, Key West.

Intelligent and educated beyond the learning of most of the pioneers in the rough frontier settlements, Cuthbert proved to be a man of many skills, noted as a navigator, fisherman, and especially hunter. He was born at the family plantation near Charleston, South Carolina, less than a decade before an attack on nearby Fort Sumter signaled the start of what Cuthbert's family called the War Between the States. One of nine boys, he grew up as a member of an aristocratic tidewater family that found its fortune swept away by the war.

Never comfortable in the highly structured society of tidewater South Carolina, George Cuthbert left the Low Country sometime in the late 1870s or early 1880s. He worked his way down to the southwest coast of Florida, arriving finally at Marco, the domain of Bill Collier. There his free spirit found a home.

In the late fall of 1889 he set out in his sloop for Fort Myers, the center of Florida's plume trade, lying directly north of Marco. In the frontier settlement on the Caloosahatchee River he purchased the supplies he would need for a long trip—food, coffee, whiskey, ammunition and gunpowder and, inevitably, arsenic to treat the plumes of the birds killed. With him aboard his sloop was first mate Will Henderson, a Fort Myers plume and gator hunter.

Cuthbert sailed down the west coast, leaving the Gulf of Mexico to enter Ponce de Leon Bay, a hundred miles south of Fort Myers. Through narrow channels surrounded by mangroves he threaded his way to the east, where he knew the rookery must lie. He reached Oyster Bay, then sailed into the Joe River, a channel that rimmed the south side of Whitewater Bay, a large saltwater bay about fifteen miles long.

Somewhere near Tarpon Creek he anchored his sloop, leaving it in the care of Henderson. From this point the going was slow and extremely arduous. Cuthbert used a small portable canoe, which he could pole or paddle. For a good part of the way he had to wade through shallow, moccasin-infested waters, pulling the boat behind him. Occasionally he had to tug or carry the boat across dry land or, worse, through mangrove thickets. He had to protect his food, water, and matches and, even more vital to his mission, his rifle and ammunition.

Cuthbert poled his boat through the narrow, shallow channel of Tarpon Creek until he reached the open waters of Coot Bay. He crossed the bay and entered a stretch comprised of mangrove thickets, marshland, and from time to time dry land, with no lakes or channels to ease his trip.

On and on he drove himself, his eyes darting back and forth between the ground and water, where poisonous snakes might lurk, and the skies overhead, where birds in flight could lead him to his pot of gold. At times he paused to climb a tree to look for the next lake, a channel, or with luck the rookery itself.

Suddenly he emerged from the mangroves. Just ahead he saw a lake. At the far end of the lake lay an island. Could this be the rookery? But as he poled his way around the perimeter of the lake, he saw no great concentration of birds.

Cuthbert knew the rookery would have to be an island with a good stand of trees for nesting, a supply of twigs for nest building, plentiful food nearby for the demanding appetites of the newly hatched baby birds, and, finally, the natural protection from predators that an island afforded. Plume birds had two principal enemies, the plume hunter and the raccoon. A rookery on a small island was safe from raccoons, since the waters surrounding it were patrolled by alligators, ever alert to coons rash enough to swim in their domain.

But no rookery was safe from hunters.

When he reached the eastern end of the lake, Cuthbert found no channel leading out. He moved back and forth before a solid mass of mangroves. He pulled his boat to the shore and scrambled up into a tree, seeking a view farther to the east. His hopes rose as he saw another lake, a small lake, no more than two hundred yards away. Laboriously, agonizingly, he pulled the boat through the thick growth of mangroves until he reached open water again.

Once more he saw islands, once more he was disappointed. He found no rookeries. But in the skies overhead he saw more and more birds in flight. At the eastern end of the lake, he encountered another solid wall of mangroves, no break, no channel, no creek. He probed and explored, but he found nothing to point the way through the thicket. He knew from the flight of birds that the rookery must be to the east. But how long could he keep driving himself? There was a limit to his food supply, to his water, and eventually to his endurance.

And then he saw it.

A white feather floated out underneath the mangroves. There was no channel, but there was an unmistakable current flowing into the lake from the east. He parted the mangroves and began to work his way through, tracing the current upstream by observing bits of debris floating by. On and on through the mangroves he waded, swatting at the mosquitoes and horseflies that hounded his every step. At last, through the thickets, he could see he was close to another lake. He brushed aside a final mangrove and stood up to look out across the blue water.

He knew instantly he had found it. It sat there at the far end of the lake, less than a mile from where he stood, a shimmering, quivering cloud of white, bigger than any other rookery he had ever seen. He could not even guess how many thousands of birds roosted there.

For a time there must have been a brief period when he simply stood there, drinking in the wonder and the beauty of the sight. He would later describe it to his children as "a flower, a beautiful white blossom."

Then he turned, went back for his boat, and dragged it through the mangroves, hacking at the roots with his hatchet when necessary. But only when necessary. He wanted to make sure no one else would find a clearly defined pathway.

Cuthbert pulled his boat into the lake and began a slow, unhurried approach to the rookery. From hundreds of yards away it greeted him, the overwhelming smell—a nauseating blend of decomposing fish, regurgitated flesh to feed the baby birds, and basic bird smell—and everywhere the bird droppings, seemingly streaking the foliage of every tree, covering the ground underfoot, even discoloring the water around the island. The stink alone would have driven away anyone but an ornithologist. Or a plume hunter. Cuthbert pressed in closer and closer.

The rookery appeared to be about two acres in size, bustling with blue herons, roseate spoonbills, white ibis, and every kind of egret—American, snowy, and reddish. By the thousands the birds flew in and out of the rookery, rising like white columns above the green mangroves. The closer Cuthbert moved, the more nauseating the smell, the louder the noise of the wings, the creaking and snapping of tree branches as birds alighted or took off in flight, the harsh *cuk-cuk-cuk* of the egrets, soon to make a terrible sacrifice to the greed of the great urban fashion centers.

Cuthbert's practiced eye told him he had arrived at the right time. The rookery was, in the parlance of the plume hunter, "ripe." The egrets were in full bloom. In the breeding season they displayed the nuptial plumes essential to courtship—and essential to the trade, essential to the design and manufacture of the most beautiful and costliest millinery creations. But "ripe" also meant that a perverse quirk of nature offered the armed plume hunter an incalculable advantage. At nesting time egrets, despite the deadly rifle fire, remained with their nests, protecting and caring for their young until the end.

Cuthbert worked with the almost silent Flobert rifle developed by the French.[3] He raised the weapon to his shoulder and fired. A stricken egret fluttered down out of the tree, attracting little attention in the noisy, crowded rookery. Cuthbert fired again. And again and again.

Who knows how long he shot? Hours? Days? Did he shoot until his boat was filled with egret scalps? Or simply till he ran out of ammunition?

Eventually he started back. He left behind a rookery littered with the carcasses of birds he had killed and scalped, food for vultures and crows and hungry gators. He also left behind nests where orphaned baby birds would slowly starve to death. Or be eaten by crows or ants.

Even with a full cargo of egret scalps in his boat, the trip back to his sloop was easier. There was no groping to find a mysterious island, just a matter now of finding his way back to Whitewater Bay without leaving behind a trail for another plume hunter.

Then he was back in his sloop again, where he had left Will Henderson only a few days before. The time had come for him to treat the plumes with arsenic to preserve them. The feathers were still many weeks away from delivery to New York milliners.

Cuthbert returned to his home on Marco Island just before Christmas

1889 and then sailed on up to Fort Myers.[4] Many buyers for the New York industry operated out of the little river port. Most were retailers who bought and sold a wide variety of items. Among their ranks were a city commissioner, the supervisor of county voter registration, the postmaster, and a noted hotelier. Plume buyer George Shultz ran the area's telegraph station and also operated the Tarpon House, a world-famous sportsman's hotel that attracted such celebrity tarpon fishermen as Thomas Edison, Henry Ford, the duke of Sutherland from Scotland, and John Jameson, a revered distiller of Irish whiskey.

Cuthbert sold his plumes to one of the town's most prosperous merchants, W. R. Washburn, who was engaged in many businesses. He sold lightning rods, ran a barber shop, and bought and sold gator hides and bird plumes.

The day after Christmas, an item on the sale appeared in the *Fort Myers Press*. "Capt. Cuthbert and William Henderson returned Saturday from a trip as far South as Cape Sable alligator and plume hunting. They brought back 147 gator hides and 265 bird plumes."

After Christmas they went back again, prepared now for a bigger harvest. The results of that second trip appeared in the paper two months later, on February 27, 1830:

"Capt. Cuthbert and mate, Will Henderson, bird hunters of high renown, sailed into our port one day last week on Capt Cuthbert's schooner with something over 900 bird plumes, having been out some six weeks. This is what we call a good haul. Mr. W. R. Washburn, the lively bird plume dealer of this city, purchased the whole lot."

The story goes that Cuthbert received the staggering sum of $1,800 for one of his two trips; the payment for the other is "unknown." What is known is that with the proceeds of his two plume hunts he purchased half of Marco Island, bought a schooner of his own, and filled his three-bedroom house with the kind of furniture he was accustomed to in the plantation home of his youth.[5] He settled down then to farm his land. After his two spectacular hunts, he seems to have turned his back on the dirty business of plume hunting.

Will Henderson was less lucky. In 1891 a fellow plume hunter shot and killed him. The motive—anger at Will's refusal to tell him the location of Cuthbert's Rookery.[6]

In his travels to Key West, Cuthbert met N. L. Barfield and his wife, son, and his pretty teenaged daughter Fannie, all from Ebeneezer, Mississippi. Barfield had planned to buy land to farm on Cape Sable. Cuthbert, who knew that desolate country as well as anyone, strongly recommended against it. Instead he talked the Barfields into moving to Marco and staying with him until they could find a place. They stayed with him long enough for George to form an attachment to Fannie's charms and her cooking. In 1894 they were married.

Cuthbert's name was given to the rookery he found and to the lake in which it lay. Neither he nor his follow frontiersmen could have known the international renown that would come to the rookery. Famous ornithologists would travel vast distances to see it. It would be recreated as an exhibit at the American Museum of Natural History in New York City. And it would become a precious jewel to be protected by a slowly emerging conservation movement.

Cuthbert did, however, become something of a local hero. In the *Fort Myers Press* he was never written about with the breezy first-name familiarity reserved for the good ol' boy plume hunters. He was always Captain Cuthbert.

As far as the paper was concerned, neither the hunters nor the buyers were villains or despoilers of a rich natural heritage. There was little environmental awareness, but there was a keen appreciation of the need for cash-poor settlers to make a living. By 1887 bird plumes and taxidermists' specimens constituted the little town's third most valuable export, producing $25,000 in revenue. Cattle, which could be seen strolling casually through the main streets, ranked first with $180,000, while sugar and molasses brought in $50,000.

The *Fort Myers Press* realized considerable revenue from plume industry ads. Some were placed by firms in the northeast, such as Otto Wagner and Lewisohn & Company of New York; W. Gouldspee of Boston, and R. Washington & Company of Baltimore. Substantial local merchants who represented the New York millinery industry also advertised regularly. A particularly large local advertiser was the prominent firm of Bain & Evans, "Dealers in Florida Curiosities, Plumes, White Egret and Pelican Skins, Alligator

Teeth and All Native Birds of Taxidermists." J. W. Bain was the local post-master.[7]

P. E. Pontier of nearby Tampa, in an ad on June 2, 1887, injected the theme of regional prejudice to try to improve his position in the plume market. "Warning," he cautioned. "Don't be deceived by parties in the North, Advertising to pay Large Prices for plumes and furs, when you Can Do Better At Home."

The paper reported regularly and somewhat affectionately on the exploits of local plume hunters. P. C. Gaines was a plumer whose name appeared frequently in the columns, for example on October 16, 1886: "P. C. Gaines has a barber shop; still scalping." And then on November 6: "P. C. Gaines fell into our arms and wept as he handed us $2.00 for a subscription Tuesday." Editor Stafford Cleveland had noted previously that Gaines and Sam Hough were "back from a plume hunt with only moderate success. Bird hunting is hard work and does not pay many of the hunters remarkably well."

Plume hunting, however, paid George Elliott Cuthbert well. The half of Marco Island that he bought with plume proceeds would be valued today in the billions of dollars.[8]

8 The Palm Beach Dudes

BY THE END OF THE 1880s the world around Lake Worth was beginning to come of age. Lantana, where the Bradleys lived, and Hypoluxo Island, where Charlie Pierce lived, were growing. And the coconuts planted on the barrier island in 1878 had induced the pioneers to give their corner of the world the name Palm Beach. But just west of the settled area, something of the old wild Florida still prevailed, and Guy and Lou enjoyed their forays into the wilderness.

The Bradleys maintained good relations with the Indians. Guy and Lou formed a plume-hunting partnership with Tommy Listee, a hefty six-footer strong as a mule. The Bradley boys furnished guns, ammunition, and small boats. They sold the plumes to such buyers as Steve Andrews, keeper of the Orange Grove House of Refuge, and split the profits three ways.[1]

Once on a hunting trip Guy and Lou found themselves suddenly surrounded on all sides by Seminoles. The boys were terrified. Then the Indians started to laugh. On the frontier it passed as a practical joke.

The Indians held both Edwin and Lydia Bradley in high regard. One day Big Tommie, another Seminole, one with a fearsome reputation, was attacked by a panther in a swamp near the Military Trail, a primitive road built a half century earlier by Major William Lauderdale during the Second Seminole War. Big Tommie had made a fire at a hammock to ward off the winter chill. He was leaning over the fire cooking his supper when the panther landed on his back. The big cat buried its teeth in Tommie's neck, tearing at his back with its claws. Big Tommie drew his knife and slashed at the panther until he struck the cat's heart. The panther died.

So weak from loss of blood he could hardly walk, Tommie struggled to the home of Edwin Bradley. The Seminole knew that E. R., who had studied medicine as a young man, was his only hope. Bradley saw that Tommie was near death. He worked quickly to stop the bleeding, then insisted the big Indian stay with the family until he regained his strength. Lydia Bradley helped nurse him through his recuperation.

"Panther eat Indian, no eat white man," Big Tommie said. The panther, Lou believed, would have killed an ordinary man, but Big Tommie had extremely large neck muscles, which saved his life. After his health returned, he went back into the Everglades west of Lantana. But he returned soon with venison for the Bradleys, his way of thanking them.

One year at Thanksgiving a group of Palm Beach sportsmen organized a hunting competition. In the scoring system a large buck counted for sixty points, a small deer forty-five, and so on, with the emphasis on the food value of the game shot. The losing side would pay all costs for the supper and dance that would follow.

Lou, Charlie, and Toney Canova made up the Hypoluxo team. The teams were to hunt all day the day before Thanksgiving and for a short time on Thanksgiving morning, then transport their game to Cap Dimick's Cocoanut Grove House by 4 P.M. The day of the hunt Charlie and Toney went by the Bradley home to meet Lou. They found him sitting with a heavily bandaged foot resting on a chair.

"Well, I cut my foot so badly I can't go hunting," said Lou. "I'm sending Guy in my place."

"If you can't go, I suppose Guy will have to do," said a crestfallen Charlie. "But you know he has not proved himself much of a hunter."

The team set out for Lake Osborne. There they boarded their skiff for the trip to Camp Everglades, their old hangout on the edge of the flat woods. At the hunting grounds they each took a separate trail and did not see each other again till sundown.

Charlie killed two sandhill cranes and two curlew for thirty points, a total with which he was well pleased until he reached the camp. There he saw Guy displaying a yearling buck he had killed and hung on a spruce tree. It was Guy's first deer, and he was proud of it. Forty-five points for Guy.

Toney later showed up without any game.

"Guy was the lucky boy, and to say he felt big at having beaten two good hunters so badly is putting it mildly," wrote Charlie. "He could not keep his face straight whenever he looked at his deer."

But the contribution of a substitute hunter was not allowed. With it, Hypoluxo would have won. Still, as a hunter, teenager Guy Bradley had come of age.

Later that season a rifle match was arranged at the Cocoanut Grove House. A large crowd of spectators gathered, dressed in their "Sunday-go-to-meeting" clothes for the supper and dance afterward. The rifle range was located on the edge of the marsh, a few hundred feet east of the hotel. The distance to the target was one hundred yards. The highest possible score for four target shots was an even twenty.

Twenty-two contestants entered. Guy's team won the rifle match. The highest individual score was eighteen, compiled by Charlie Pierce—and eighteen-year-old Guy Bradley. Their team was called the Palm Beach Dudes."[2]

Music was a Christmas present that had entered the lives of Guy and Lou Bradley on December 25, 1880. Settlers in the lake country gathered on the grounds of the Cocoanut Grove House, the first Palm Beach hotel. After a day of feasting, Cap Dimick, the owner, held a dance in the hotel's dining room, the first dance ever held on the lake. A new family, the Brelsfords, supplied the music—violin, cello, and organ. This was the first time the Bradley boys and Charlie Pierce had heard what they called "real music." That night they made up their minds that someday they would own violins and learn to play them. Someday.

Guy's grandfather Asa Bradley promised to send Guy a violin from Chicago. Five years later he made good on the promise. Meanwhile, Charlie located a fiddle in Jupiter.[3]

Guy proved to be a fast learner. Wrote Charlie: "He took to it like a duckling takes to water. In a few weeks he was playing a few pieces fairly well. Then we commenced to play together with Mrs. Bradley playing accompaniment on her guitar."

London-born Lydia Bradley served as the catalyst that created the Hypoluxo String Band. A trained musician herself, she gave lessons to Guy and Charlie and taught Lou how to play a twenty-five-dollar cello, which he bought with money earned by extra trips as a barefoot mailman. Lou was slow at learning music, so his mother had to stay with the band in the early days to keep Lou in tune. Later Guy assumed the task of tuning Lou's cello.

One night E. M. Brelsford asked the boys to take over for his group at a dance on Palm Beach. Brelsford's violinist and trombonist, Charles Lane, who had been a member of the Seventh Regiment Band of New York City, gave them advice on how to play for dancers:

"Time, time, just give them time, that's all they want. It doesn't make any difference what kind of tune you play, so long as it has the right time."

After that night, the boys agreed the "right time" had come to go public with their musical talents. Regular practices, three times a week, sharpened their skills. When the next dance was held, the Hypoluxo String Band was ready—Guy on first violin, Charlie on second violin, and Lou on cello, with Mrs. Bradley still on guitar to keep Lou in tune. The band played for every dance the rest of the winter.

By the winter season of 1888 the band had shown real improvement. Charlie learned to play the cornet, George Lyman replaced him as second violinist, and Lou was ready to play without his mother's watchful eye. One night at a dance at the hotel, the band played from eight o'clock until the dance broke up at three in the morning, then they sailed back across the lake to their homes. In the fall of 1892 the Hypoluxo String Band played for its last dance at a housewarming for M. B. Lyman's new store in Lantana.

Music had brightened more than a few lives, promising something more than farming, hunting, fishing, and boating. Farming in the heat of south Florida was an exhausting, repetitious chore. Fishing and hunting were less fun when a badly aimed shot meant a meager dinner table.

"To the women in pioneer days the problems of food and housekeeping were greater even than the loneliness and work," wrote Lillian Voss Oyer, Charlie Pierce's niece, years later. "This was made more difficult because almost without exception the families who came to South Florida were from cities or towns. They were accustomed to all the conveniences of that time."

But times were changing. In 1886 the first school was built on Palm Beach, and in 1889 an Episcopal church, Bethesda-by-the-Sea. Cap Dimick had a large impact on the lives of the people around the lake, and particularly on the Bradley family.[4] Dimick, active in Democratic politics back in his native Michigan, noticed that the settlers along Lake Worth had cast more votes in the 1888 election than those who lived along Biscayne Bay. The unincorporated area on the bay, generally referred to as Miami, served as the county seat of Dade County. In those days Dade County stretched from the Upper Keys to the St. Lucie River, an area containing 7,200 square miles but only 726 residents. Why, asked Cap, was Miami the county seat when Lake Worth was home to more voters?

Dimick and his colleagues agreed on the unincorporated village of Juno on the north shore of Lake Worth as their choice for county seat. Since Juno would soon be the southern terminus of the short-haul Jupiter and Lake Worth Railroad, already under construction, it would be relatively easy to reach from the north by railroad and from the south by boat. On February 19, 1889, voters went to the polls, and a heavy vote in the north of the county seemed to indicate a convincing victory for the Lake Worth faction. The Juno group, however, were wary of Miami chicanery, so they took three brawny souls—who would be described these days as "muscle"—with them to guard against any problems when the votes were certified. Leading this strong-arm group was Patrick Lennon, an Irishman chased out of the British Isles for his efforts at chasing England out of Ireland.[5]

Juno won, 107 to 80, but victory was not going to be all that easy. The Juno gang picked up word that Miamians would use force the next day to keep the county seat from being moved north. The Juno group fled Miami that night spiriting the county records out in an Indian dugout canoe. They fled north on Biscayne Bay, then took Snake Creek back into the Everglades to scare off any pursuers. Finally they arrived back in Juno and a new era began.

Soon the tiny county seat attracted the first newspaper ever published on the lower southeast coast. Guy Metcalf, who owned the *Indian River News* in Titusville, moved his weekly paper to Juno, the city of the future, and re-named it the *Tropical Sun*.[6] Edwin Bradley, who had acquired newspaper experience in Chicago, joined the *Sun* staff as a columnist.

Bradley's columns were written under three different names. One appeared under the pen name Ruthven, which was his middle name. Another ran under "OMB," which stood for Old Man Bradley, and a third under "The Sage of Lotus Cove," as he was known with some affection. He wrote with a jaunty, light touch and seldom missed a chance to publicize the activities of his two sons. In early 1892 he reported that Captain Guy Bradley had charge of a big sloop, the *Oliver*, which had sailed to the inlet to unload a schooner. The boat was carrying lumber for a house for Cornelius Vanderbilt Barton of Palm Beach. Another column told of a twenty-four-hour hunt to the west of town by Guy and George Charter. Guy killed "a fine young buck and turkey which patrons of the Coconut Grove Hotel pronounced very good."

In the spring E. R. wrote about an upcoming wedding party: "The '4 M's' went moon-shining a few nights ago with a little party aboard. A romantic spirit took possession of the craft. She disappeared the next day and we learn she means to change her name. At Lyman's she is now donning white wings and after the ceremony will be called the *Saucy Lass.* The wedding trip will be to Biscayne Bay and Key West. Best man, Mr. Albert Robert; ushers, Hearst and Patterson; mate, Guy Bradley. There are whispers that oat flakes, cooked in a double broiler, will be served at the supper."

Guy was beginning to mingle with people of importance in the area. The bride- and groom-to-be were Miss Byrd Spilman and Fred Dewey. Fred and Albert Robert would play significant roles in the flowering of Palm Beach, soon to emerge as America's most prestigious winter resort. Byrd would achieve an independent fame. An animal lover, she wrote a book about pets called *The Blessed Isle and Its Happy Families.* Her father, a minister, wrote the beloved Christmas carol "Away in a Manger."

In the late spring of 1892 the *Tropical Sun* reprinted a lengthy obituary of Asa Bradley, Guy's grandfather, from a Chicago paper. The local paper's introduction to the obit indicated that Asa Bradley owned considerable property in Dade County and had visited the section in the past.

In the late summer of 1892 Captain Guy Bradley, now twenty-two, acquired the job of delivering the mail from Hypoluxo to Juno, a distance of roughly twenty miles. He carried the mail across Lake Worth in the Bradley family boat, the *Rosie B,* named after the elder of Guy's two sisters. Ruthven wrote an item about Guy's delivery prowess: "P.M.'s [postmasters] are growling because the mail boat arrives ahead of the usual time. Tow a skiff, Guy."

Young Guy was also taking care of his relations with the lake's power structure. Guy Metcalf, already a force in the community, wrote in his paper: "Guy M. Bradley of Lotus Cove made a flying business visit to Juno yesterday. We found a bag of limes in our office as a memento of his presence. Come often, Guy."

On September 8, 1892, Guy's father made the news columns himself, putting his strong Democratic Party connections to good use. A brief note announced that he had been named superintendent of schools for Dade

County, selected for the post by the Dade County School Board. For a wild frontier society groping toward some semblance of civilization, the position was one of considerable responsibility. Yet the job, which he held until 1895, was only part-time, leaving Edwin free to write columns, raise fruits and vegetables, and sell Davidge's fertilizer at a price of twelve dollars a ton. The pay for the most important educational job in the county was less than four hundred dollars a year.

At this period the Bradley family was finally enjoying a measure of prosperity. Edwin was making what the *Sun* called "a considerable addition to his dwelling house." In November the *Sun* announced a dancing party to celebrate the completion of "his new house." Even more significant was the brief announcement that "Guy Bradley, the hustling mail carrier, has had a house built, land cleared and 600 pine [pineapple] slips set out on his homestead and his brother Lou has had the same done to hizzen."

On December 1 Guy made his last trip as mail carrier between Hypoluxo and Juno. "Guy Bradley and his sailboat *Rosie B.* have been efficient coworkers and will be missed," wrote his father. "We have never had any better mail service on the lake than they have given us. But lots of things, people and institutions have had to step down and out to make way for the steam engine to give better service and Guy goes with the rest. With his pluck and energy it's very probable he will soon fill an important position elsewhere."

A week later OMB gave out the good news: "Guy has been promoted to be a Captain and General. He will run Mr. Albert Robert's naphtha *General Factotum.* He has secured a fine position."

For the first time in his young life Guy enjoyed an income of his own. His earnings came from a variety of sources. He worked as a farmer, a mailman, and a boatman. And as late as 1892 he was still augmenting his income with an occasional plume hunt.

Metcalf branched out by winning a contract from the county to build the first road between the lake country and Biscayne Bay.[7] It was to start at Lantana and terminate at Lemon City, a little to the north of the settlement on the Miami River. Charlie Pierce had been hired to inspect the proposed site for Metcalf's road. He planned, as he put it, "to kill two birds with one stone" by combining his inspection trip with a plume hunt at a rookery he had located in a swamp about two miles north of Boca Raton.

For his combined plume hunt–inspection trip Charlie engaged the services of Edwin Bradley's mule and an expert "muleteer" named Guy Bradley.[8] The two friends left early one morning from the Bradleys' home in Lantana and arrived on the north bank of the Hillsboro River just before dark. The next morning they waded through the swamp to the island where the plume birds were nesting.

"We remained at that place for a day and a half and by that time had killed all the birds in the rookery," Charlie wrote.

Then they moved on, looking for more nesting places. Just north of a large lake they saw a bird fly out of a small island about a hundred yards out in the swamp. The boys were reluctant to wade out that far for just one bird. The question was: Were there any other birds on the island?

"We can mighty soon find out if there are any more birds in there by firing a shot into it," said Charlie.

"Try it," Guy replied.

"I'm afraid that old mule of yours will not stand the report of the gun. He might become frightened and bolt."

"Oh, I can hold him all right. You go ahead and shoot."

Charlie aimed his gun toward the island and pressed the trigger. No birds rose from the island. But the mule took flight—the beast reared up on its hind legs, whirled suddenly, throwing Guy to the ground, and bolted off toward home.

Guy bounced up immediately and ran after the mule. "Whoa, whoa," he cried. The mule never slackened its pace. The woods resounded with the rattle and clank of the cooking utensils strapped to the mule's back, mixed with the sound of Guy's futile cries.

Charlie followed, picking up pieces that shook loose from the mule in its mad dash for home. He retrieved a pail of butter, a frying pan, and a coffeepot. Soon he too looked like a fully loaded pack animal.

Then he saw Guy coming back, leading the mule. Guy hitched the mule to a tree and flung himself down on the ground without a word.

"How far did you run before you caught him?"

Guy, leaning back against the tree with his eyes closed, wearily replied: "Oh, about a mile farther on, and I am just about played out. Let's camp here for the night. I feel right now like I could stretch out and rest for a week."

"All right, but it is some distance to water. I suppose you could drink a bucket full yourself right now. It will not be hard to carry that much. But it's too far to carry all that the mule will need. We will have to lead him to the swamp to water him."

"No, sir," said Guy. "That mule is going to stay hitched right where he is now, all night. I am not going to give him anything to eat, either. I'll teach him that to run away from me means something. I'll not give him any water or feed tonight. Just to punish him."

"All right, it's your mule. You can do as you please with him, but I don't believe the mule will understand he is being punished."

But, like a mule, Guy was stubborn, a trait he would continue to display throughout his life. The animal received no food or water.

Guy's treatment of the mule proved counterproductive. A wry comment from Ruthven in the *Tropical Sun* read: "Guy Bradley has been amusing himself for some days hunting for a stray mule."

Although Ruthven/OMB/Sage of Lotus Cove continued to write about his family, he also used the power of the press to give voice to various complaints about the world around him. For example, he objected to jury duty at his busiest season. He made the somewhat exaggerated claim that his time was worth fifty dollars a day when he was setting out eggplants and tomatoes. Apparently the law was not impressed. One week later the list of jurors included ERB.

Ruthven wrote of preparing land to raise eggplants—and red spiders. The reference to insects set him off on an attack on the railroad's freight rate differential:

I have always found that the worst insects I had to contend with were common men and railroad directors. You can spray them with a solution of concentrated cuss words; you can saturate them with a compound extract of human kindness, or sprinkle them with tears wrung from the long suffering husbandmen and still they will charge you $33.33 freight per ton for vegetables to Jacksonville and they will only charge you $4.50 per ton for the fertilizer to raise them with. Consistency, thou art a jewel, black as tar. Don't you see that it costs more to haul freight north than it does to haul it south? I'll tell you why; it surely costs more for the trainsman to stop at a 4 dollars a night hotel in Jacksonville than it does in a cheap Titusville boarding house; hence the distinction in freight, hotel and insects.

In blasting the railroads, Bradley little dreamed that one day he and his son Guy would go to work for the man who built the railroad. Edwin by now was ready to move on to another job, if his item of May 12, 1892, is any indication:

"I have hunted industriously for more ease all my life but am still at the bottom of the ladder, writing squibs for a country newspaper."

The job he added to his résumé was a prestigious one—superintendent of schools. But it was only part-time, so he continued to hunt "industriously."

9 Sharpshooter

IT WAS TEN O'CLOCK that night when the sound of the big guns began to shake Richmond, the Virginia capital. Ten o'clock, the night of April 9, 1865. From across the James River, the Union troops fired a hundred guns, a deafening salute. The echoes of the artillery died away, then the bands blared out. For the city of Richmond they screamed forth a humiliating message: "The war is over. Lee has surrendered."

The weary troops of the South had fought—and lost. Defeat and disillusion lay like a morning fog across the tired city. And nowhere was it worse than at Chimborazo Hospital, a maze of wooden buildings where convalescent Confederate soldiers tried to regain some measure of health. The rambling hospital city of Chimborazo, reputed to be the world's largest medical facility, spread out over forty-five acres. It looked down on the city of Richmond to the west. Seventy-five thousand wounded and dying soldiers passed through its cottages during the bloody conflict.[1]

One of these was Walter Smith, a soldier from New Bern, North Carolina. He was recovering from a gunshot wound in his left arm and a powder burn in his left eye. He was just twenty-two years old.[2]

As a boy of eighteen, Walter had enlisted on the sixteenth day of April, 1861, just four days after the Confederates fired on Fort Sumter. His service, and the war, lasted not quite four years. And as it wound down, he knew the helplessness, the emptiness of staring at the ceiling and realizing that the cause was lost. There was nothing more he could do about it.

Walter had been assigned to Company I, Third North Carolina Regiment, CSA, under the command of General A. P. Hill. Smith had been with Hill when his army crossed the Potomac to save the day for General Robert E. Lee in one of the bloodiest battles in a bloody war. Twenty thousand casualties in one terrible day at Antietam, Maryland. But Smith fought on, at

Fredericksburg, at Chancellorsville, where Stonewall Jackson fell. As a scout and sharpshooter, he had been with Hill through the Shenandoah Valley campaign. His sharpshooting skills would stay with him.

West of Chancellorsville lay a vast region of tangled forest and underbrush bearing the ominous name the Wilderness. For two days in May of 1864 the forces of Lee and Grant fought almost blindly in the dense, dried-out thicket. The guns of war set the dry underbrush afire, and wounded men lay scream-ing in the flames that would end the war for them. Casualties in the frighten-ing battle soared to nearly thirty thousand men. One of these was young Walter Smith. A bullet tore through his left arm, destroying part of the bone, and a powder burn blinded him in his left eye.

General Grant pressed relentlessly toward Richmond, and Lee maneu-vered to meet him again at Spotsylvania Court House. "I propose to fight it out on this line if it takes all summer," Grant wired Washington. The armies clashed again at Spotsylvania. Four more days and nineteen thousand more casualties.

Smith saw no more of the action as Grant tightened the screws of war. From a hospital bed at Chimborazo, he learned that his commander, A. P. Hill, had been killed at the long siege of Petersburg, one week before the war ended.

At war's end, Smith was honorably discharged from the CSA at Chim-borazo Hospital. He had joined the battle a raw youth, enlisting on April 17, 1861, for six months. At one time he held the rank of first sergeant but had to accept the rank of private when he re-enlisted. He left the war a tested, battle-hardened veteran of the bloodiest combat Americans had ever waged. Tough though he was, his spirits sagged as he looked ahead to his prospects. A South impoverished by a losing war could offer him no opportunity. Where could he go? Back to Craven County, North Carolina? Life there had been less than ideal before. His parents were dead; he had had to live with uncles.

Before the war he had been a seaman, had even visited far-off Washington State. He had sailed around Cape Horn, the worst experience of his life, he claimed, worse even than the war. Still, the sea was what he knew. He had lived most of his life near the water, near the mighty Cape Fear River at Wil-mington and near the Neuse River that flowed past his home town of New

Bern, the old colonial capital of North Carolina. Always at home on a sailing vessel, Smith decided his best chances lay with the sea.

Sometime around 1870, the year Guy Bradley was born, Smith's boat sailed into a treacherous storm off the Carolina coast. The crew labored to save the ship. They failed, and in the terrifying struggle a wave swept Smith overboard. A strong swimmer, he fought to stay afloat. Somehow he managed to make it to land. He collapsed on the beach. No one knows how long he lay on the sands. A family living on a sea island not far from Charleston found him there, unconscious. He was close to death from pneumonia and exposure. They took Smith into their home on the barrier island and nursed him back to health. Walter Smith was a survivor.

"What can I do to repay you?" he asked.

"Can you read and write? Do sums?"

He nodded.

Smith lived for several years on the island, teaching the children. It couldn't last. He was young, strong, and restless, and the island's confinement offered him no opportunity.

In time he found his way over to the South Carolina mainland to the town of Honey Hill, close to the Santee River in Berkeley County. He met a girl named Nancy Rebecca Brinson. When she married Walter on the twenty-fifth of April, 1878, at the little town of Palmerville near Moncks Corner, she was only fifteen. He was thirty-six. He called her "daughter." She called him "Captain."

They lived first with Rebecca's uncle Isaac Wilson. The story persisted that Isaac had found an old trunk containing enough pre-Confederate money to keep the family going for a while. The Smiths invested part of this treasure trove in a schooner. Sometime in the 1880s they moved farther down the coast to the fishing village of Brunswick, Georgia. There Smith earned a living by oystering. In Brunswick their first child, Tom, was born in 1888. Seventeen years later Tom's adolescent wildness would trigger a tragic event.

In the 1890s a smallpox epidemic struck Brunswick. Smith, now the father of two small children, decided the time had come to leave Georgia. Thirty miles to the south lay the Florida border. Below the line stretched some four hundred miles of sparsely settled frontier land, its desolation broken by only occasional populated areas. The largest of these, Jacksonville, was located just south of the border. Smith, already familiar with the northern coast of Florida, picked Jacksonville as his destination.

Smith sailed his schooner out through St. Simons Sound. As he cruised past Jekyll Island, he could see its wharf and fancy clubhouse, its tower dominating the flat seaside landscape. Jekyll Island was already beginning to attract a colony of rich "swells" from the north. Smith did not realize it at the time, but he was heading for another colony of rich "swells." On down the coast he cruised past Cumberland Island, past Florida's northernmost port, Fernandina on Amelia Island, and entered the St. Johns River.

"Where you from?" they asked him as he reached the port of Jacksonville.

"Brunswick," said Smith.

"Can't land here," he was told, "at least not without quarantine."

For three weeks the Smiths anchored out in the harbor, well back from the town. Along the way the captain got tired of waiting. Jacksonville, he concluded, was not the place for the Smith family.

Smith sailed back out into the Atlantic and proceeded to work his way farther south. It was a wild, unsettled seacoast he found below St. Augustine and Daytona Beach. He sailed past the Canaveral Lighthouse, past the huge rookery on Pelican Island in the Indian River lagoon, past the Gilbert's Bar House of Refuge near the St. Lucie Inlet. Then, looming ahead, he saw the towering red column of the Jupiter Lighthouse, guarding a treacherous inlet.

A little south of Jupiter he sighted another inlet, this one a bit more hospitable. He steered his schooner through the pass and into the calm, protected waters of Lake Worth. Here he found a number of small settlements—Juno, the Dade County seat, on the north end of the lake, Palm Beach on its the eastern shore, Hypoluxo on an island to the south, and to the west the settlements of Lake Worth and Lantana. Smith sailed down the west side and tied up at Morris Benson Lyman's dock in Lantana.

Smith liked what he saw, a waterfront community not far from a good inlet, yet protected from the Atlantic's heavy seas. There was a bustle, too, about the place, heavy construction under way, particularly over on Palm Beach. Smith could see that the lake was a place where things were happening.

He liked the people he met. Among these were the Bradley family, people of substance in Lantana. The father, Edwin, was the county superintendent of schools. And Rebecca Smith and Lydia Bradley formed a strong friendship right from the start, bound to each other in part by a love of music.

Thus in 1893 the paths of Captain Walter Smith, aged fifty-one, and Captain Guy Bradley, twenty-three, finally crossed. Friends at the start, they were destined to become the deadliest of enemies.

10 Flagler Takes Charge

ALERT AS A HAWK, the tall, gray-haired man gazed intently from the deck of his luxury steamer at the rich growth of coconut palms rising from the sandy barrier island to his west. He liked what he saw—a navigable inlet and, just to the west of the slender strip of land, a large blue lagoon ideal for boating and fishing. And palm trees, palm trees everywhere, courtesy of an 1878 shipwreck.

Memories of the isle of palms on the southeast coast of Florida stayed with him after his return to his base in St. Augustine. A year or so later, in either 1888 or 1889, he returned to the island called Palm Beach. This time he went ashore. He made detailed notes on the topography, on existing structures and on the owners of the island's most promising properties.[1]

It was a game Henry Morrison Flagler liked to play, sizing up a situation for himself without revealing his identity. He had often worked this way in the past, back when he and his partner John D. Rockefeller were building their mammoth industrial empire, Standard Oil of Ohio. The spectacular success of their company had armed Flagler with enough money to do whatever he liked with the rest of his life. Now his visionary mind propelled him forward into not just a second career but a whole parade of new careers: railroad builder, hotel tycoon, developer of farming "colonies," steamship magnate, and creator of world-renowned luxury winter resorts. He was sixty-two years old when he decided to push his railroad down the southeast coast and into the land of eternal summer. There in the subtropics he would transform the island of coconut palms into an American Riviera.

In 1890 his railroad reached only to Daytona Beach, already emerging along with Ormond Beach as a popular winter resort. Why go any farther? Only a sprinkling of hardy—some would say foolhardy—pioneers lived south of Indian River country, which lay just a short distance below Daytona's hard-packed sands.

Whatever southeast Florida promised, few could see it. But Flagler could. The visionary's eye saw palm trees ruffled by balmy, tropical breezes, the rich red of bougainvillea in blossom, and overhead a cloudless winter sky. Flagler knew he could lure a new land's new millionaires to his hedonistic island. Think what it would mean to the wealthy to spend their winters at the beach while unwashed legions struggled to grind out meager livings amidst snow and ice. During the sunny days they could fish the Gulf Stream or the calmer waters of Lake Worth, or hunt deer or bear in the woods west of town, then feast that evening at his elegant hotel dining rooms.

But first, Flagler understood, his guests would need a comfortable, even luxurious, way to journey to Southeast Florida. And second, they would need resort hotels, with wide porches, waterfront vistas, fine restaurants, and elegant ballrooms for parties and balls. Who but Flagler had the vision, the money, and the boldness to open up a country as wild as a Central American jungle?

In 1892 the Great Man made the decision to thrust his railroad some hundred and fifty miles to the south, to the little-known western shores of Lake Worth, just across from the barrier island its handful of residents had obligingly named Palm Beach.

To start his grand scheme, Flagler decided to acquire a one-mile-square section about four miles south of the northern tip of the island. On the side facing Lake Worth he planned to build a large resort hotel and a railroad bridge to the mainland. On the eastern side, facing the Atlantic, he would build cottages and perhaps a second luxury hotel.[2]

As his land agent, Flagler picked Guy Bradley's friend Albert Robert. In February 1893 the Bradleys and their neighbors began to pick up rumors that the tycoon would soon be coming to the area. It was said that somewhere along the lake he would select the site for a luxury tourist hotel. Landowners wondered if their property would be blessed or even be close enough to his acreage to enjoy the warm glow of heightened property values spreading like the ripples from a coconut falling into the lagoon. Then in March came word to the sparsely settled lake community that the time was near. The tycoon would arrive the next day.

Albert Robert chartered Charlie Pierce's *Oriole,* a twenty-eight-foot sloop, to escort Flagler and his party around the area. For three days Flagler studied the land on Palm Beach. He showed no interest in any other area. The prime piece of land he wanted was owned by Robert McCormick, a wealthy businessman from Denver. On it McCormick had built Sea Gull Cottage, a large wooden residence, the finest in Palm Beach.

"Buy it," Flagler told Albert Robert.

The agent bought the McCormick property for $75,000, a staggering sum by the Palm Beach standards of 1893. Flagler would make it his Palm Beach home for nearly a decade. He spent an additional $225,000 to expand his holdings to a hundred acres, much of the land purchased from the Albert Geer family. On this land he picked the site for his luxury hotel. It lay on the west side of the island looking out across Lake Worth. Albert Robert also paid $50,000 of Flagler's money for a point of land owned by E.M. Brelsford, fiddler and operator of the town's general store. At Brelsford Point, Flagler would eventually build his great mansion, Whitehall.

On the west side of the lake, across from Palm Beach, a $45,000 investment bought the land on which Flagler would create the new city of West Palm Beach—or, as it was first spelled, Westpalmbeach. It would serve as the terminus for his railroad and as the town "for my help."

Real estate formerly unnoticed jumped in price to $150 and then to $1,500 per acre. Old pioneer homesteaders on the island suddenly found themselves rich. Flagler told Robert to pay whatever the owner asked, no matter what it cost. He was not interested in land speculation, or in delays. Later he said, "I have not bought any land at Palm Beach with the expectation or desire to sell it again. As a matter of profit, I think I can make more in one week in Wall Street than I can make in one year in real estate in Florida."

Flagler's arrival changed the lake country forever. As plans progressed for his Palm Beach hotel, his Florida East Coast Railway moved farther and farther south, past Cape Canaveral, past the old Seminole War military post called Fort Pierce, on across the St. Lucie River, closer and closer to the Loxahatchee River, where the Jupiter Lighthouse stood.

He tried to buy the Jupiter & Lake Worth Railway, better known as the Celestial Railroad because it connected Juno and Jupiter. Intoxicated by the prices Flagler was paying for land, its owners demanded a large amount. Unfortunately for them, Flagler had bought other railroads. He considered the Celestial's asking price exorbitant. Instead of caving in to their demands, he built his road farther to the west. In the process, he doomed the little line and the town of Juno to extinction. Within three years the Celestial Railroad was in bankruptcy. By the early 1900s a bypassed Juno was no longer the county seat, reduced instead to a ghost town's lonely decline.[3]

In stunning contrast, Flagler's plans for his hotel assumed grandiose proportions. What he envisaged was nothing less than the world's largest resort hotel. And he wanted it right away. To build it, his contractors, Joseph A. McDonald and James McGuire, needed hundreds of able-bodied adult workers, yet the total population around the lake was no more than two or three hundred people, including women and children. Droves of black laborers were brought in, many from the nearby Bahama Islands. They were paid $1.10 an hour, slightly higher than the national average wage for unskilled labor. Tents were erected and shanties built to house the "colored" laborers. Their village, just north of the hotel site, was called the Styx, a strangely poetic reference to the river at the entrance to Hell.

Others in a workforce that grew to a thousand were housed at what had once been Palm Beach's ultimate resort hotel, the Cocoanut Grove House. Flagler leased the hotel from Commodore Charles J. Clarke, a wealthy Pittsburgh transportation magnate who had bought the property from Cap Dimick. Cap's pioneering forays into tourism had proved successful in the relatively primitive days of the lake. He wisely concluded his small, modest hostelry could never compete with the sophisticated luxury of a Flagler hotel. Dimick sold out and became a banker, a druggist, and eventually Palm Beach's first mayor. The following October Cap watched sadly as the Cocoanut Grove House, the first hotel on Palm Beach, caught fire and burned to the ground.[4]

Meanwhile Flagler pushed ahead with the development of West Palm Beach, the workers' town, as he called it. James E. Ingraham, one of his key executives, laid out the town with downtown streets bearing such botanical names as Banyan, Clematis, and Datura. The Flagler organization was striving mightily to have both the hotel and West Palm Beach ready when the railroad came to town. Henry made it a race between railroad and hotel builders. The hotel people won.

The Royal Poinciana opened on February 11, 1894, just nine months after work began, an incredible construction feat. Flagler named his huge hotel after an exotic tropical tree with blossoms so extravagantly red that Jamaicans call it the flamboyant. Ironically, the flame tree blooms only in the summer, so the guests at his hotel, open only in the winter, could never gaze upon its beauty.

Still, he gave them other things to see and do. When all wings were completed, the hotel's three miles of corridors promised brisk walks to 1,081 rooms, capable of accommodating 1,750 guests in luxury. At the Royal Poinciana even the chamber pots were trimmed with gold. The hotel's dining room could seat 1,600 people, served by 400 waiters. Guests could enjoy golf, tennis, fishing, and boating. Like all new Flagler hotels, the "Ponce" was painted a bright lemon color, a tint destined to be known in South Florida as Flagler yellow.

On April 2, 1894, the train reached West Palm Beach. By the start of the 1894–95 winter season Flagler was ready for the arrival of the rich and famous in their luxuriously appointed private railroad cars. Vanderbilts, Whitneys, Carnegies, great names in society and industry, quickly made Palm Beach the "in" winter resort.

The barrier island would never be the same. Perhaps the first to feel the change were the blacks who had built the hotel. Once their work was completed, Flagler did not want them living in shacks and tents just north of the grounds. The story persists that he lured the workers to West Palm for a barbecue, then burned the Styx to the ground while they were away celebrating with food and drink. It is more likely that he simply moved them to the mainland, then burned down the shacks to make way for what would prove to be another lucrative subdivision in Flagler's town.[5]

One who saw the change firsthand was fiddler Guy Bradley. No longer would there be any call for the down-home dance music of the Hypoluxo String Band. Now fancy society orchestras and singers were brought down from New York to entertain the "swells."

Another change was the arrival at Palm Beach of women of fashion, ladies who had no need to garb themselves in the plain, practical raiment of pioneer women. Beautiful gowns and hats decorated with plumes were now seen in the lake country. Guy and others who shot birds could see for themselves the fruits of their marksmanship. The wearers of the hats were unlikely to connect the flowering of fashion with the nondescript plume hunters they might encounter on a West Palm Beach street, should they dare to venture into the rowdy town built for Flagler's help.

The main difference Flagler had made to most of the lake people, however, was blessed relief from their austere, cash-poor subsistence economy. Lake dwellers could now make a decent living. Stores had customers who could buy. Farmers, commercial fishermen, and market hunters could sell food to the huge restaurant at the "Ponce." And boat captains like Guy found more work transporting people and cargo.

In the midst of the rejoicing on the lake, personal tragedy again struck the Bradley family. Their daughter Rose, just seventeen, died in Lantana; her brief obituary gave no cause of death. She was the second of the Bradley girls to die, a little over a decade after the family lost Flora at the Fort Lauderdale House of Refuge. Rose's death left the saddened Bradley parents with two sons, Lou and Guy, and just one daughter, Margaret Emily, better known as Maggie, now fifteen.

Guy's father was particularly intrigued by Flagler's new order. Edwin Bradley never stayed long at any job. During his administration as superintendent of schools, he had been in charge of eleven school centers, spread out over a sprawling, sparsely settled county. His school system contained 130 mostly unenthusiastic pupils and 11 teachers whose annual salary averaged $220. As county school superintendent, Bradley himself never earned more than two-thirds of the $600 a year the barefoot postal route had paid him.

In April 1895 he resigned from his post as the county's top educator to join the vast Flagler organization. E. R. became assistant superintendent of the Florida Coast Line Canal and Transportation Company, one of many companies Flagler used to open up South Florida. The company was engaged in dredging the East Coast Canal, later renamed the Inland Waterway and still later the Intracoastal Waterway.

Guy was well connected with the Flagler interests. He had served as mate aboard the boat that took the Fred Deweys to the Keys on their honeymoon; Fred became Flagler's secretary. And as captain of Albert Robert's naphtha launch, Guy was close to Flagler's advance man on the lake.

By 1895 the sixty-five-year-old Flagler was on his way south to the settlements on Biscayne Bay. In early 1896 his railroad reached the New River, where a handful of people had settled near the location of the first Fort Lauderdale, built in 1838 during the Second Seminole War.

On April 22 the railroad arrived at the north bank of the Miami River. Some three hundred people, mostly Flagler employees, turned out to greet Flagler and the first train. Three months later the residents decided to incorporate. They wanted to call the city Flagler. Henry demurred and threw his support to the faction that wanted to name it after the river that flowed into Biscayne Bay. Miami, an Indian word meaning "sweet water," had an exotic, picturesque sound to it, a good name for a subtropical resort. As was invariably the case, the residents did what Flagler wanted. They called it Miami.[6]

The same year the railroad reached Miami, Flagler formed the Model Land Company.[7] Its mission was to develop and sell the enormous tracts of land he was acquiring from the state in return for opening up the frontier with his railroad and canal. At eight thousand acres for each mile of track, Flagler was able to claim more than two million acres of state-owned Florida land, a substantial part of it in the Cape Sable area. To run the company that would develop these enormous landholdings, he named James E. Ingraham as president.

Ingraham had formerly worked for Florida's other major railroad man. Henry Bradley Plant had toyed with the idea of extending his tracks across the Everglades, from Fort Myers to Miami. Ingraham had drawn the difficult assignment of conducting the survey across the River of Grass. At Fort Myers he had been told his journey would be hampered by a series of deep lagoons with a large central divide, or even a huge unknown lake basin. Instead he found a seemingly endless wet prairie of sawgrass, which tore the skin like the scrape of a saw. Ingraham and his crew endured sore feet, dwindling food supplies, and exhaustion. When they asked an old Indian woman how long it would take to reach Miami, she laughed and said: "Indian, two days. White man, fifteen."

Finally they found an Indian in a canoe who helped them make their way out of the maze. They reached the headwaters of the Miami River, shot the stream's rapids, and found themselves in the little settlement on Biscayne Bay. Following his ordeal Ingraham made a rather predictable recommendation to Plant: Do not build a railroad across the Everglades.

Flagler heard about Ingraham's survey, conferred with him, then brought him into his organization. In addition to running the Model Land Company, Ingraham was responsible for advance planning for new railroad routes, the accumulation of technical data, and the establishment of new towns along the railroad. He also developed a program for promoting the Flagler interests through advertising, brochures, and a magazine called the *Florida East Coast Homeseeker*. After the creation of the Model Land Company, Edwin Bradley was transferred from the canal company to the new development enterprise headed by Ingraham.

At about the time E. R. Bradley first went to work for Flagler, Kemp Burton and his family, originally from Michigan, moved to Linton, a new settlement just beginning to spring up along the track south of Lake Worth.[8] It would later change its name to Delray Beach.

Burton had a mule named Bill, which attained considerable local fame. For one thing, as the only mule in Linton, his services were much in demand. More important to his celebrity status, however, was his attire. In the muck land near Linton, Bill was inclined to sink into the ground after heavy rains. Because he needed to keep Bill and his plough busy, Kemp tied boards to each of Bill's feet and called them "muck shoes." To protect Bill against mosquitoes, Burton made trousers for his legs from gunny sacks, tied other sacks around the mule's middle, and on his head placed a straw hat with two holes cut out to accommodate his ears.

Kemp Burton had a son who was also named Bill. Since Kemp Burton used fertilizer sacks to clothe his mule and the Bradleys sold fertilizer, this may have been the first connection between the two families. Whatever brought them together, Bill the man became an important figure in the life of the Bradleys. After serving in the Spanish-American War in 1898, he married Maggie Bradley and remained close to Guy for the few remaining years of his brother-in-law's life.

Meanwhile Ingraham was moving ahead with plans to develop farming colonies on the Flagler holdings—not just along the existing tracks but also in areas the railroad might serve in the future. Sooner or later Flagler's rails would be pushed to the end of the country, to the island city of Key West, perched out in the ocean at the tip of the Keys. Would the tracks head southwestward along the Keys, or would they cut across the Everglades to Cape Sable, then cross Florida Bay via a causeway?

The time had come, Ingraham decided, to develop the company's Cape Sable holdings. In 1897 he picked Edwin Bradley to serve as the Model Land Company's land agent for the cape colony.

Why was Bradley willing to forsake the genteel society that had finally brought a measure of comfort to the lake country? His wife was certainly happy in the increasingly cultural world that was developing along the lake. In 1896 the Ladies of Palm Beach published *The Lake Worth Historian, a Souvenir Journal* to raise funds for the Royal Poinciana Chapel on Palm Beach. Lydia Bradley wrote a piece titled "Truck Gardening," which among other observations spoke glowingly of Dade County tomatoes: "Of all the crops that are grown here, the tomato is the most beautiful. The plants grow so luxuriantly, and their soft green leaves contrast so well with the soil, whether it is red, gray or black. . . . A visit to one of these fields is a pleasure that is not soon forgotten."

E. R. Bradley had lived there in the Lake Worth country for two decades. He and his family had seen it evolve from a primitive community where earning a livelihood was an unending struggle against starvation to a world of opportunity and civilized niceties. He would subject his family now to life in a hot, buggy, unhealthy environment harsher than the lake had been in its wildest days, more remote, more lawless, and infinitely more lacking in the comforts of day-to-day living.

One incentive was money. As part of the deal, the Bradleys would be able to acquire large properties on Florida Bay. If Flamingo became the railroad terminus, they could look forward to considerable wealth. If not, Edwin Bradley would still have an affiliation with the most powerful company in Florida.

Others wondered if perhaps the move was rooted in Edwin's restlessness. "When the school and the church got too close, it seemed like it was time for Edwin Bradley to move on," Charlie Pierce's sister Lillie once said.

By moving, Bradley eliminated a minor confusion that had arisen in the Palm Beach area. In 1898 a second E. R. Bradley moved to Palm Beach. The differences between Edwin Ruthven Bradley and the other E. R. were substantial. The newcomer was Colonel Edward Riley Bradley, who proceeded to open a gambling casino that became internationally famous and operated for nearly half a century, an illegal casino so successful its betting limits were even higher than those in Monte Carlo.[9]

In the months leading up to the move to the cape, Edwin committed the greatest blunder of his life. He persuaded Captain Walter Smith to leave the lake and join the Bradleys in Flamingo. Smith's party would be a large one— the captain and Rebecca, her brother Dan Brinson, and the Smith children, Tom, Mamie, Danny, and little Ed, an infant. Late in the summer of 1898, as the Spanish-American War was ending, the Smiths sailed out of Lake Worth on their schooner, the *Cleveland,* into the Atlantic and on down to the frontier village of Flamingo.

1. Tourists cruising on the upper St. Johns River amused themselves by shooting at alligators on the banks and birds in the trees, as shown in artwork in the October 3, 1874, issue of *Harper's Weekly.* Courtesy Florida State Archives, Photographic Collection.

2. Guy Morrell Bradley, in his early thirties. Courtesy Luther "Buddy" Roberts.

3. Hardly a "tropical paradise," the first Pierce house on Hypoluxo Island was home for a while for the Bradley family. On this site would later stand the estate of Consuelo Vanderbilt, who for a time was the duchess of Marlborough. Courtesy Historical Society of Palm Beach County.

4. The highest
prize for the
plume hunter was
"Little Snowy,"
the snowy egret.
Courtesy Florida
State Archives,
Photographic
Collection.

5. White ibis in a South Florida rookery.
Courtesy Historical Association of
Southern Florida.

6. Florida plume hunter displaying a
yellow-crowned night heron, probably
shot on Santa Fe Lake. Courtesy
Florida State Archives, Photographic
Collection.

7. J. H. Batty. Courtesy American
Museum of Natural History.

8. Cuthbert Rookery, mid-twentieth
century. Courtesy Florida State
Archives, Photographic Collection.

9. George Elliott Cuthbert, in his mid-forties. Courtesy Cornelia Cuthbert Deas.

10. Schoolhouse in Palm Beach, with sixteen-year-old Guy Bradley *(far right)* dressed up neatly for a photograph. Courtesy Historical Society of Palm Beach County.

11. Henry M. Flagler. Courtesy
Historical Association of Southern
Florida.

12. Typical Flamingo house at the time
the Bradleys lived on Cape Sable.
Courtesy Historical Association of
Southern Florida.

13. A dapper Kirk Munroe. Courtesy
Historical Association of Southern
Florida.

14. Uncle Steve Roberts. Courtesy Historical Association of Southern Florida.

15. Miami got a glimpse of a well-plumed hat worn by one of its best-known residents, Mrs. James M. Jackson, wife of the pioneer doctor for whom Jackson Memorial Hospital was named. Courtesy Florida State Archives, Photographic Collection.

16. Guy Bradley proudly wearing the badge. Courtesy Historical Association of Southern Florida.

17. Post office at Cape Sable.
Courtesy Vincent Gilpin Jr.

18. Cuthbert Rookery exhibit created
at the American Museum of Natural
History in New York by Frank
Chapman. Courtesy American
Museum of Natural History.

19. The Jefferson Hotel, where Guy
Bradley first met William Dutcher.
Courtesy Florida State Archives,
Photographic Collection.

20. Guy Bradley in the rowboat in
which he made his final journey out
to Oyster Keys. Courtesy Vincent
Gilpin Jr.

21. Senator Hunt Harris. Courtesy Florida State Archives, Photographic Collection.

22. Fronie Bradley and the two Bradley children, Morrell and Ellis. Courtesy Ferguson Addison.

23. An aging Walter
Smith and his wife,
Rebecca. Courtesy
Edwin Smith.

24. Audubon representa-
tive Charles Brookfield at
Guy Bradley's grave.
Courtesy Historical
Association of Southern
Florida.

11 The End of the World

THE SEMINOLES HAD avoided the area for years, fearful of a giant serpent some said guarded the desolate mosquito-haunted land. The white man, too, was slow to move into Cape Sable country. In 1884 an enterprising Key Wester named James A. Waddell ignored the myths, took advantage of the low price of Cape Sable land, and established a 1,120-acre coconut plantation along the East Cape waterfront. It lay just to the south of the route Cuthbert took in finding the fabled rookery that made him a rich man. Waddell managed to hire a few workers to tend the plantation. Not many lasted very long.

After Cuthbert's discovery, the fear of the unknown lessened. Hardy plume hunters and the occasional ornithologist like Scott began to follow the plume birds to the cape. Scott had come to see the only large flock of flamingos known to nest in the United States. He wrote an unflattering description of the countryside:

> Eighteen miles east of Cape Sable are three bays. . . . the water in these bays is extremely shallow, being rarely more than eighteen inches in depth, while the average depth on ordinary tides probably does not exceed six inches. The bottom is soft and muddy, and the mud is very deep, making wading impossible. The shores are wooded with black mangroves, buttonwood and some cabbage palmettos. The land is so low as to be flooded at any extra high tide. The country is . . . the home of the mosquito in all its varieties. Even in February, when I visited the region, though a stiff easterly breeze was blowing all the time, going ashore was something to be dreaded. It was a most desolate and forbidding region either on sea, if sea it may be called, or on the land."[1]

Slowly plume hunters, optimistic farmers, fishermen, drifters, and renegades began to locate in the area. In 1893 Duncan Brady, far from his native

Nova Scotia, came to the cape to manage the Waddell coconut plantation. Since he owned his own sloop, he also hauled cargo between the Keys and coastal settlements on the mainland. Brady soon concluded the time had come for a post office.[2]

First, the government told Brady, give the place a name. No name, no post office.

Brady picked Flamingo, a tribute to the beauty the dazzling pink birds brought to the area. Fewer than fifty people lived at the cape, most of them rough-hewn misfits. Yet when asked to approve the name for their community, they turned from their scurvy ways to back Brady's sensitive aesthetic choice. They agreed to call their frontier outpost, a huddled group of shabby driftwood and palmetto shacks, Flamingo. The village's first postmaster was Howell Cobb Lowe, who doubled as Flamingo's justice of the peace.

Two ironies soon appeared. As the settlement grew in size and firepower, the flamingos deserted the cape to return to the West Indies where they could find friendlier nesting places. And some of the residents shortened the name of their village to Mingo. Others playfully stretched it out to Fillymingo. Still others, striving for a measure of cynical accuracy, called it the End of the World.[3] It was about as far away from civilization as any American could run. And many in the shabby waterfront village were running from something—the law, their wives, old enemies, or sometimes just responsibilities. It was a place where few questions were asked. Or answered.

The southernmost settlement on the United States mainland, Flamingo perched at the tip of Florida's nearly impenetrable Everglades, roughly ten miles east of East Cape Sable and about the same distance to the southwest of Cuthbert Rookery. The outpost fronted on Florida Bay, a body of water so shallow that even skilled boatmen had trouble navigating its treacherous shoals, as W.E.D. Scott had written. Across the bay from Flamingo lay the Florida Keys, a string of mostly small islands stretching 150 miles from Biscayne Bay to the island of Key West, South Florida's largest city, with a population of some seventeen thousand people. Key West, the county seat of Monroe County, was a good sixty-five miles from Flamingo.

When the Bradleys arrived in the late summer of 1898, they found a familiar face at the Flamingo post office. Walter Smith, the old sharpshooter, had already made his considerable presence felt in Cape Sable country. Smith had reestablished the village post office, discontinued since 1895, and gotten himself named postmaster.

Smith, in fact, had learned his way around the area so well that he had a proposition ready for the Bradley boys.[4] His sons were too young to help him shoot birds in any large quantity. His oldest, little Tommy, was just ten. Why not work with Guy and Lou, both of them seasoned plume hunters, both of them young men on the lookout for ways to bring home extra money? With the Bradleys aboard, Captain Smith skillfully maneuvered his schooner *Cleveland* through the treacherous shoal waters of Florida Bay to Oyster Keys, roughly two miles offshore.

As they approached the two small islands, Lou and Guy saw cormorants, hundreds of them flying in and out of the rookery. The dark brown birds dove into the waters of Florida Bay, using their hooked bills to catch fish with a skill that roused the envy of the most proficient angler. Squawking noisily, they returned to the rookery on Oyster Keys. Unlike most large birds that feed on fish, the cormorants, particularly as squabs, were considered tasty morsels in Key West, where they sold for a quarter apiece.

Smith's proposition was to form a partnership in which all three shot cormorants, then transported them to Key West using either the fifty-three-foot *Cleveland* or the Bradleys' boat *Pearl,* a forty-foot sharpie. Both boats were well suited to the shoal waters of Florida Bay. The profits were to be split three ways.

It was a deal Guy and Lou were reported to have accepted. Easy money, it seemed on the face of it. There was no way any of the three could have foreseen the tragedy that lay ahead at Oyster Keys.

Now twenty-seven years of age, a strong, healthy Guy Bradley was eager to get on with his life. Far in the past was his sickly childhood. As skipper of the *Pearl,* he commanded a considerable measure of respect. At Cape Sable he also became a man of property. A quarter of a mile of waterfront land was his, eighty acres for a house and a farm. He could plant vegetables, sugarcane, and fruit trees. He could even get married and raise a family of his own. That is, if he could find an attractive, available young woman in as desolate an outpost as Flamingo.

Hunting, of course, would continue to be a source of food and income, as it was for every able-bodied male in pioneer country. Cash could come from plume hunting. Every plume hunter had heard tales about Cuthbert Rookery, but the hunters had also heard that the birds were growing scarcer with each passing season, and this they could see for themselves.

Kirk Munroe had told the Bradleys many stories about how the plumers had ruined the rookeries, how the skies once colorful and noisy with birds were now silent and empty.

"I don't think in my reincarnation, if there is such a thing, that I want to come back to Florida," said the author, who lived in Coconut Grove. "They are killing off all the plume birds. I remember when the spoonbills on the beach in front of my house made such a racket it was almost unpleasant. Now they are all gone—they never come back anymore."

The Bradley family had first met Kirk and his wife Mary in 1883, in the days when the Munroes lived briefly on Lake Worth. They were an unlikely couple to find on the frontier, well educated, well read, well informed. Kirk, a Yale graduate, wrote articles for such prestigious American magazines as *Harper's Weekly* and *Scribner's*. During the 1890s he became the most popular author of juvenile fiction in the country. Mary Barr Munroe, likewise a lively intellect, was the daughter of a British novelist.

The Bradleys had kept in touch with Munroe as his fame grew. The writer traveled all over the state, savoring the wild outdoors, always seeking material for his books and articles. He canoed through the swamps and the Everglades, sailed through the Ten Thousand Islands, camped with the Seminoles. He saw the glorious wildness of the frontier land slipping away as "civilizers" claimed it from the birds, the animals, and the Indians. Among his many titles were *Canoemates: A Story of the Florida Reef and Everglades* (1893) and *Big Cypress: The Story of an Everglade Homestead* (1894).

The Munroes, who spent part of each year in New York, mingled with the leaders of the emerging conservation movement. On their return they brought back to South Florida the environmental ferment accelerating across the states to the north. George Grinnell, the big game hunter and magazine publisher who created the first Audubon Society in 1886, teamed with a noted hunter named Theodore Roosevelt to establish the Boone and Crockett Club. Its goal was to preserve big game animals in the American West. Naturalist John Muir organized the Sierra Club to protect the mountain wilderness of California. Another publisher, G. O. Shields, formed the League of American Sportsmen to work for "bag limits." From the pages of his *Recreation* magazine this crusading publisher, who had blasted away with bullets at virtually every kind of game animal in this country, turned to blasting away with words at "game hogs" and "fish hogs." He published their names in *Recreation,* relegating them to his "hog pen."

And in 1896, in the midst of a conservation groundswell fueled by "macho" big game hunters, the Audubon Society was revived by a Boston society woman, Mrs. Augustus Hemenway.[5] It resurfaced not as a national organization run by Grinnell's magazine but as one small state unit, the Massachusetts Audubon Society, run primarily by concerned women who knew where to apply the pressure. Hats with plumes were worn by fashionable women of means, "ladies" Harriet Hemenway knew quite well. She saw them as people she could talk to about styles in headgear. Soon after Massachusetts revived Audubon, the movement began to reach out across the country.

Thus Guy Bradley, who had killed his share of plume birds, began to have second thoughts about his destructive pursuit. When he and Lou and Charlie Pierce were kids, it had been fun to test their marksmanship as the birds flew in and out of the rookeries, chattering and squawking cheerfully along the way. But now the fun was giving way to doubts. And not just for Guy Bradley.

On Chokoloskee Island on Florida's west coast, Charles G. McKinney ran a trading post noted for its colorful motto: "No Banking. No Mortgaging. No Insurance. No Borrowing. No Loaning. I must have cash to buy more hash." The influential Sage of Chokoloskee tried plume hunting just once. His mentor was a famous plumer, Gregorio Lopez, an immigrant from Barcelona, Spain. With sadness and disgust McKinney wrote not just about the killing of the egrets but also of the nests left behind by the death of the adult birds: "The crows would go and take the eggs and carry them away and eat them. It looked hard for me. I decided I didn't think it was doing God's service and I never went on that kind of hunt any more."[6]

Gregorio, however, was not converted. Long after plume hunting was made illegal in Florida, he continued to hunt the birds in Central America and eventually gained legendary status with a creative smuggling scheme. He once brought back to the United States a large shipment of plumes skillfully concealed inside a mattress aboard his boat.[7]

Still, the ideas from the great cities of the North were slowly invading the remote corners of even a very deep South, and huge changes would soon follow. In the life of twenty-seven-year-old Guy Bradley some very important changes were close at hand.

In 1898 a huge change was signaled by the arrival in Flamingo of a schooner from Apalachicola on Florida's northern Gulf Coast. The schooner, bound for Key West, tied up at a dock on Florida Bay. Aboard the schooner were the two Vickers brothers, Almon and Shelly, their mother, Rebecca, and their pretty, hazel-eyed, brown-haired sister, Sophronia.

Fronie, as she was called, was a jolly, outgoing eighteen-year-old who laughed freely. Prospects became even more pleasing when a smitten Guy Bradley learned that the Vickers family was moving to a city on his regular boating run. The city was Key West.

By the end of 1898 Florida, which had served as a military staging area, was adjusting to the end of the Spanish-American War. Bill Burton, a friend of the family from Lantana days, returned from the war and married Guy's sister Maggie. Burton was ready now to play a major role in the affairs of the Bradley family.

And Guy was increasingly enthusiastic about his trips to Key West, particularly to a boarding house established at 638 William Street by Fronie's mother. He discovered among other things that the shapely, good-natured Fronie was an excellent cook and, surprisingly, a woman who was handy with boxing gloves. He also learned that her last name was not Vickers. Her full name was Sophronia Vickers Kirvin. She was, however, no longer married.

Was she a widow, whose husband had been killed in the Spanish-American War or in an accident aboard a commercial fishing vessel, a major industry in the Panhandle area where she had lived? Had there been a divorce, a rare occurrence in the 1890s South? Or had she, backed up by her family, simply fled from a failed, possibly abusive marriage? Or had it been only a common-law marriage, from which a woman could simply walk away without the red tape of a court hearing? To her surviving descendants her Kirvin ties remain a mystery.

Whatever the explanation, Guy kept up his pursuit, traveling to Key West as often as he could. A sturdy, attractive young man of twenty-eight, generally well liked, he had found the woman he wanted to marry. Just the opposite of the vivacious Fronie, Guy was serious, introverted, and shy. But shyness in a man can be an appealing trait to many women. Fronie apparently thought so, for she consented to marry Guy.

On May 12, 1899, the Reverend Charles W. Frazier performed the marriage ceremony at the First Congregational Church of Key West.[8]

The couple moved into Guy's modest place on the Flamingo waterfront and set about making a home for themselves. A hard worker, Guy stayed busy, piloting the family boat on cargo runs in the Keys, tending to his small farm, and surveying for the Flagler Model Land Company.

Guy also rented a small house on Newton Street in Key West. Fronie wanted to be closer to her family, and particularly her mother, after she became pregnant.

Their first child, Morrell Bradley, was born in their Key West home on September 29, 1900. They soon learned that the arrival of children can put a strain on the finances of a young couple.

12 The Patriarch

IN THE SUMMER OF 1901 Guy Bradley witnessed two events of note, one a hurricane that struck the Cape Sable shore in mid-August, the other the arrival in Flamingo of one Stephen Lyons Roberts. The hurricane was mild and of little consequence. The same description did not apply to Steve Roberts.

Uncle Steve, as the patriarch would quite properly be called, would in short order become the "boss" in Flamingo. The magic of the Flagler connection had failed to deliver that lofty status to Edwin Bradley. Mingo's primitive society recognized force of character. Edwin lacked it. Uncle Steve radiated it like a cluster of Cape Sable mosquitoes, buzzing everywhere and into everything. One of the Mingo residents drawn into the wiry little man's net was Guy Bradley. Guy's pathway into the Roberts faction came through Uncle Steve's sons. Gene and Loren Roberts became Guy's best friends in a thin community where best friends were hard to find.[1]

Steve Roberts's leadership traced back to genes packed with a classic American blend of authority and violence. His father, Albert G. Roberts, was a veteran Indian fighter and surveyor. After the close of the Mexican War, he settled in Micanopy in Alachua County. Albert operated the first large sawmill in the state. His surveying skills came into play when he laid out the new city of Gainesville, just north of Micanopy.[2]

On June 24, 1850, Albert's wife, Ann Elizabeth Mizell Roberts, gave birth to Steve. On his mother's side the child inherited the blood of the Mizells, one of Florida's most prominent pioneer families. Ann's grandfather served as an Alachua County commissioner. Her father, David Jr., was the first chairman of the Orange County Commission and the first sheriff of Orange County, which had as its seat the new town of Orlando. Her brother John was a prominent judge and one of the leading Republican politicians in

Florida. Her first cousin Morgan Bonaparte "Bone" Mizell became Florida's most famous cow hunter, as Florida cowboys were called.

The Mizells gained great power in central Florida after the Civil War. During Reconstruction the Republican Party captured control of the state for the first time. John Mizell was named judge of the Orange County civil and criminal courts, and David, Steve's grandfather, was appointed sheriff.

Bitterly opposed to the Mizells were the Barber family. Their family feud dated back to eighteenth-century North Carolina. In late-nineteenth-century Florida, the current head of the clan, Moses Barber, had several wives, each separated from the other by a two-day cattle drive. In May of 1869 he was convicted of polygamy and fined five hundred dollars. Another conviction for confining and imprisoning a man against his will followed shortly.

The Barbers' anger at a justice system controlled by two Mizell brothers, John and David, exploded the following February. Sheriff Mizell, his brother, and his son were heading across Barber rangeland on official business when a single gunshot rang out. The sheriff fell from his saddle. Minutes later he was dead.

The assassination touched off the bloodiest range war in Florida history. Judge John Mizell immediately formed a posse and went after the Barbers. By summer six Barbers had been killed, five by gunshot wounds and the sixth by drowning, a fate influenced heavily by a plowshare tied around his neck before he was thrown into Lake Conway in Orlando. Officially, all six deaths were classified as "shot while attempting to escape arrest." Moses, the leader of the clan, fled the area, after first telling his various wives they were free to claim his land and cattle in the Kissimmee area.

One thing was clear. The Mizells knew how to take care of their interests.

Young Steve Roberts was learning the ways of the violent world in which he would live. As a youth of twenty, Steve would have been a member of the posse formed by his uncle John. He certainly must have stood in the good graces of the Mizell family. Less than two years after the range war ended, Judge John Mizell, who now carried two guns, officiated when Steve married Dora Drawdy on January 14, 1872.

It was said of Steve that he "married well." The Drawdys were people of substance. Both Lake Dora and the town of Mount Dora were named after his bride's mother. As a dowry, Dora brought a herd of cattle to the new family. Unfortunately, the cattle drowned in a hurricane that flooded Roberts Island, in eastern Orange County. Still Steve and Dora lived on their ranch and orange grove at Roberts Branch until 1898. At this point their family doctor, a relative named George Crawford, ordered Steve to take Dora to the seacoast to live.

"It'll help her ward off the consumption," he told Steve. Tuberculosis, he noted, was prevalent in her family.

The doctor had ample opportunity to observe Dora's condition. Steve's sister Ola operated one of Florida's largest illegal whiskey stills. "Dr. Crawford," a relative observed, "was called in at various times to make a study of the quality and yield of one of Ola's largest stills which operated near there. I'm almost sure it was the biggest producer this side of Jacksonville."

What a sight it must have been, covered wagons filled with Robertses, headed out across a wilderness without any defined roads, only a few cattle trails and footpaths.

"Uncle Steve and Dora and Hilton Brown [another relative] and Old Man Will Drawdy and several others and a whole lot of half grown kids all took covered wagons and headed for Cape Sable via Punta Gorda," Allen Taylor, a Roberts descendant, wrote.

To reach the phosphate port of Punta Gorda, roughly 120 miles away, the Roberts caravan followed the Peace River, a watercourse well known to Florida cattlemen.

"I don't have any idea how long it took," Hilton Brown, one of the "half-grown kids," said later.

The slow, uncomfortable journey through the Peace River Valley showed them a Florida that was beginning to change. In 1886 the Florida Southern Railway reached Punta Gorda. Towns like Fort Ogden and Arcadia began to spring up along the way. Arcadia was the base for Ziba King's cattle empire, which boasted as its foreman Dora's first cousin, the free-spirited, free-spending Bone Mizell. The artist Frederic Remington, visiting Arcadia in 1895, had painted a picture of Bone that ran in *Harper's Weekly*.[3] Unlike the "macho" cowboys Remington had painted in the American West, Bone was a joker who used a quick, sharp wit to cover his unfortunate lisp. He sometimes lit his pipe with dollar bills and was known to drink too deeply of a cheap and potent booze called Jamaica ginger. Once he rode into a saloon and took his first drink before dismounting from his horse. Another time, after he passed out in a saloon, his cow hunter pals dumped him in a graveyard, built a circle of fire around him, then poked him with sticks to wake him up. Said Bone: "Dead and gone to hell, 'bout what I expected."

But the range was changing. Phosphate was discovered in the valley, and mining became the money industry. Conveniently located on the shores of a large bay called Charlotte Harbor, Punta Gorda became a busy port for shipping phosphate, widely in demand by the fertilizer industry. Charlotte Harbor was popular too with wealthy tarpon fishermen, many of whom stayed at the fancy resort hotel the railroad had built. Some of the Punta Gorda Hotel's early guests included W. K. Vanderbilt, Lord Warwick from England, John Wanamaker, the Philadelphia merchant prince, and financier Andrew Mellon.

At Punta Gorda Steve bought a schooner, which would be their means of traveling farther down the southwest coast in search of warmer coastal weather for Dora. Summer squalls prevented them from venturing into open water. At Jug Creek Shoals just off Patricio Island, in Pine Island Sound, summer winds drove them aground. At low tide the schooner heeled over, but they were able to refloat their boat and drift to deeper water after the tide came back in.

They sailed then to a site known as Burnt Store, a trading post burned down by the Seminoles in 1848. But to Steve the place had a different and special meaning. The party made camp in an old abandoned house. Next morning Aunt Meller Winegord gathered an apron full of seashells. Steve led them in a group about two hundred yards to a big pine tree and showed them a grave.

"This is where my father is buried," he said. Aunt Meller placed the seashells on the grave of Albert Roberts.

Uncle Steve's father had met his end in an ignominious way. In 1888 he was working on a government survey. The surveying crew was also doing a little plume hunting on the side. To preserve the plumes, the surveyors treated them with arsenic, which they carried in a Rumford Baking Powder tin. One day at Burnt Store, Albert Roberts made a batch of hoecake bread.

He used the wrong baking powder tin. The rest of the crew, all younger men, survived the deadly hoecake. Albert, a man of advanced years, died. He was buried in a solitary grave there at Burnt Store on Pine Island Trace.

By 1901 Steve and his family had advanced farther south to the upper reaches of the Shark River. From there they ventured even farther south to Whitewater Bay. There, one morning, they thought they heard the lowing of a cow, a pleasing sound to an old cattleman like Steve. He started out on foot to investigate. Late in the day he emerged from the woods and found himself staring across a prairie at a handful of shacks built on stilts facing a large body of water. He had reached Flamingo.

Roberts was invited to settle at Flamingo, probably by Edwin Bradley, whose job it was to increase the population of the place. Steve was given detailed instructions on how to reach Flamingo by boat. It was suggested he sail out of the Shark River into the Gulf of Mexico and approach the settlement around the cape and into Florida Bay.

The arrival of the Roberts entourage was a major event in the short lifetime of the town. For one thing, they had a large impact on the settlement's density. Steve and Dora had brought with them her father; five sons, Eugene, Loren, Ward, Jim, and Melch; three daughters, Florence, Ola, and Bernice; a cousin, Hilton Brown; and Aunt Meller Winegord.

Guy quickly made friends with Loren and Gene, the two sons who were closest to his age. Most people at the cape liked Steve Roberts. There was a decided measure of affection in the nickname Uncle Steve. But people could sense that, like his Mizell ancestors, he was not a man to trifle with.

"The Robertses were feared but not necessarily disliked," one observer who knew them well remarked.[4] One who did not like them was Walter Smith. He had already become a dominant figure in the community, and quite accurately he saw Steve Roberts as a major rival.

The extended Roberts family acquired land to the west of Flamingo beyond the Robert S. Douthit property and immediately set about raising sugarcane. Sugar gave Mingo settlers two pathways toward a cash return, one legal, the other illegal but seldom bothered by the law. They could manufacture syrup for sale at Key West or they could use the sweet squeezings to distill the potent moonshine "Cape Sable agerdent," a Mingo pronunciation of the Spanish *aguardiente*. In time Uncle Steve became the area's leading bootlegger.

The Robertses were willing to take extreme measures to protect their sugarcane. One year the cape settlement was beset by a horde of rats that destroyed most of the sugar crop. Sugar mill and bootlegging operations came to a standstill. Watching several cats idly mauling a dead rat, Gene Roberts came up with a bold idea.[5]

"Boys," he told his friends at a hastily called meeting, "we've done everything we could think of to get rid of the rats, but it ain't done no good. No use in us spending any more money on poison—them rats would rather eat our sugarcane. These few cats we got here has done the best they can, but they can't eat but so many rats. So I say we ought to chip in and run down to Key West and buy up a whole bunch of cats and bring 'em here."

Gene took up a collection, then set sail for Key West. A sign reading "Will Pay 10 Cents Apiece for Every Cat Delivered to This Dock" brought him a cargo of four hundred lively cats to transport back to Fillymingo.

"That trip was the worst I ever made," said Gene. "Them durn cats fought and yowled all the way."

Finally he reached Cape Sable and put the cats ashore. They bounded off in all directions and soon became as wild as the wildcats in the area. But they killed off the rats.

Steve Roberts was no stranger to the violent institution of political assassination. His grandfather had been gunned down in Orange County. In the late summer of 1901 another political assassination occurred which had even the remote village of Flamingo talking. On September 6 President William McKinley was visiting the Pan-American Exposition in Buffalo, New York. As he reached out to shake the hand of Leon Czolgosz, the anarchist fired two shots into his body from a concealed revolver. Eight days later President McKinley died.

Theodore Roosevelt, popular hero of the Spanish-American War, was sworn in as the twenty-sixth president of the United States. His elevation to the highest post in the land would give new impetus to the nation's conservation movement.

Czolgosz, who confessed to an urge to kill "a great ruler," was electrocuted.

Closer to home, Henry Flagler was putting into motion a plan that would have profound impact on the town of Flamingo. The Great Man had decided the time had come to extend his railroad to Key West. The big question remained: Which route to take?

Flagler assembled a team of engineers under the direction of William Krome. Their mission was to explore the possibility of running the railroad from Homestead to Cape Sable and then for thirty-three more miles via a causeway across Florida Bay to Big Pine Key and finally down the Lower Keys to the island city.

Krome organized a crew of surveyors to begin compiling the data for his final evaluation. One of the surveyors who worked on the project was Guy. A tall royal palm tree at Seven Palm Lake became a register signed deep in the jungle when Guy carved an inscription:[6]

G.M.B. Jan 31, 1901, 12 M, for F.E.C. Land Co.

13 A Matter of Law

IN 1897 BIRD PROTECTIONISTS in the capital of America's millinery industry had followed the lead of Harriet Hemenway and formed the New York Audubon Society. Its officers were a prominent Manhattan attorney, Morris K. Jesup, president; Miss Emma H. Lockwood, secretary-treasurer; and Frank M. Chapman, chairman of the executive committee. One of the group's vice presidents was Governor Theodore Roosevelt, already a staunch conservationist.[1]

Chapman was fast emerging as a leader in the cause. In 1899 he financed and launched *Bird Lore,* a bimonthly magazine that bore the motto "A bird in the bush is worth two in the hand." His bizarre millinery bird count on Manhattan's Ladies' Mile in 1886 had evolved by 1900 into the Audubon Christmas Day Bird Count.

Still, despite its strong executive firepower, the society got off to a shaky start. In 1899 the society met at the American Museum of National History. The *New York Times* report poked sly fun at them: "About 150 persons were present, most of them women, and fully three-fourths of the women wore birds, or parts of birds in their hats."

The following year the organization began to make progress, according to a June 3, 1900, account in the *Times:* "The women who listened to the talk of Frank M. Chapman on 'Birds of Fashion' at the fourth annual meeting of the State Audubon Society at the Natural History Museum yesterday afternoon, went home vowing that never again would they wear anything but the feathers of the ostrich on their hats." Chapman shocked them with horror stories of a shipload of ten tons of wings of willow grouse killed for their plumage, of birds slaughtered by the hundreds of thousands, and of white herons gruesomely scalped by plume hunters. Since Chapman was a skilled photographer, his already eloquent speech was made even more compelling by pictures.

In his illustrated talk Chapman told of visiting the largest ostrich farm in the country, located in Jacksonville, Florida. He explained to the audience that feathers could be removed from ostriches without pain or the bloody death that was the fate of the egrets.

A highlight of the meeting was a letter from Governor Roosevelt, commending the society for its educational work. He wrote: "Half the beauty of the woods and fields is gone when you lose the birds. To net out all the fish from the streams and to kill off half the game birds is not much more sensible than to kill milch cows and brood mares."

Already chairman of the AOU's bird protection committee, William E. Dutcher also began to represent the AOU with the state societies, as chairman. He noted that progress lagged in many states and suggested that state societies band together to exert more influence nationally. They took him up on his suggestion and in 1902 established the National Committee of Audubon Societies. They went a big step farther and named Dutcher their first chairman.

In many ways he seemed an unlikely candidate to lead a crusade for bird protection. He was not a big game hunter, as many early conservationists were, not an outdoorsman who lived on a country estate surrounded by fields and woods, not a wealthy dabbler with ample time and money to pursue his enthusiasm of the moment. He was rather a no-nonsense, businesslike, middle-aged New York City dweller who worked hard to earn a living by selling Prudential Life Insurance. He was also a bird lover.

The silver-haired Dutcher spent more unpaid hours than he could afford, constantly attacking the feather trade on both supply and demand fronts. One thing was certain. Dutcher was in the right place. Although Paris reigned as the world capital of the millinery trade, New York was the unquestioned fashion leader in the rambunctious, energetic republic that was just now beginning to pop its buttons as an international power. By 1900 the millinery industry already employed some 83,000 workers, most of them women.[2]

At every turn Dutcher's eyes were assailed by the sight of plumed hats. Aigrettes, the ultimate in style, maintained their popularity, but he had noted how fashion's whims kept endangering new birds. For example, in the winter of 1886, when the AOU had began to make its presence felt to a broader public, both grebes and imported parrots were popular, worn with furs and turbans. By summer peafowl and birds of paradise were in vogue. In 1893 whole pigeons decorated hats to be worn while strolling. Their wings and feathers were seen in the summer on golfing hats and as part of fashionable horse-show costumes.

The milliners used any birds that flew within the range of their gunners and netters. Dutcher wrote in Frank Chapman's *Bird Lore* about a list compiled by an ornithologist while taking a short trip in a Madison Avenue horsecar: "The car contained thirteen women, of whom eleven wore birds as follows: (1) heads and wings of three European starlings; (2) an entire bird (species unknown), of foreign origin; (3) seven warblers, representing four species; (4) a large tern; (5) the heads and wings of three shore larks; (6) the wings of seven shore larks; (7) one half of a gallinule; (8) small terns; (9) a turtle dove; (10) a vireo and a yellow-breasted chat, and (11) ostrich plumes."

The devastation wrought by the craze was as close to Dutcher's world as Long Island, the species endangered as commonplace to him as an actuarial table. Between Coney Island and Fire Island lay marshes, meadows, and low-lying islands, long the breeding place of thousands of common terns or sea swallows. On the beaches the least tern and piping plover laid their eggs and hatched their young. By the late 1880s Dutcher was describing the area as "a waste place, for the hand of the destroyer has left behind lone remnants of what was once a teeming colony."

Dutcher, born in Stelton, New Jersey, in 1846, had little formal schooling, since he had to go to work when he was only thirteen. He had, however, been successful in the insurance business and brought to his new task high intelligence and considerable skill in working with people. At Dutcher's death in 1920, the noted ornithologist T. S. Palmer observed that "energy, sincerity, sympathy and a remarkable tenacity of purpose were some of the characteristics which enabled him to overcome obstacles that would have disheartened a less determined man and made it possible to score success under conditions that seemed to invite nothing but failure."[3]

When he assumed the chair of the new Audubon organization, he declared: "The object of this organization is to be a barrier between wild birds and animals and a very large unthinking class, and a small but more harmful class of selfish people." In *The Audubon Ark: A History of the National Audubon Society*, Frank Graham Jr. wrote that Dutcher did not regard either the plume hunters or the hat wearers as the prime villains in the tragic drama, regarding them rather as "the large unthinking class." His prime targets, the "small but more harmful class of selfish people," were the leaders of the millinery industry who exploited both the plumers and the buyers of feathered bonnets. Education and legislation would be the keys to solving the problem.

One of the toughest obstacles facing the new chairman was Florida. The largest concentration of plume birds lay in the vast Everglades, but Florida was a state without a law to protect them. In May of 1901 Dutcher traveled to Tallahassee while the Florida state legislature was in session. He had never before ventured into La Florida, the Land of Flowers. It was a primitive state, still in its pioneer stages, according to the United States Census Florida guidelines. It ranked in 1900 as the country's thirty-third least populated state, with just over a half million residents.

It could be a hard sell, but Dutcher had some impressive support. The Florida Audubon Society, formed in 1900, was a strong one, including in its membership Frank Chapman, who wintered in the Sunshine State; T. S. Palmer, assistant chief of the Biological Survey, United States Department of Agriculture; the Reverend G. M. Ward, president of Rollins College, in Winter Park; and James E. Ingraham, a major executive in the Florida empire of Henry Flagler, who was himself a patron of the society. Honorary vice presidents included President Theodore Roosevelt, former president Grover Cleveland, and W. S. Jennings, governor of Florida.

Probably Dutcher's most important connection was Robert W. Williams, Jr., an attorney who had moved to Tallahassee in 1882 and begun to study the birds of the area the following year. He became the AOUs' Florida representative and wrote articles and notes for ornithological publications. It was Williams who directed Dutcher to W. Hunt Harris, the state senator from Monroe County. Fortunately, Harris was a rising power in the Florida State Senate and probably the most powerful politician in Key West, the county seat for the vast wilderness area that was clearly Dutcher's greatest concern.

Senator Harris skillfully secured the passage of Chapter 4357, "An Act for the Protection of Birds and Their Nests and Eggs, and Prescribing a Penalty for any Violation Thereof." The act, passed on May 28, 1901, states in part:

No person shall, within the state of Florida, kill or catch or have in his or her possession, living or dead, any wild bird other than a game bird, nor shall purchase, offer or expose for sale any such wild bird after it has been killed or caught. No part of the plumage, skin or body of any bird protected by this section shall be sold or had in possession for sale. . . . Any person who violates any of the provisions of this act shall be guilty of a misdemeanor, and shall be liable to a fine of five dollars for each offense, and an additional fine of five dollars for each bird, living or dead, or part of bird, or nest and eggs possessed in violation of this act or to imprisonment for ten days, or both at the discretion of the court.

From his trip to Florida, Dutcher had secured passage of an essential law. And in addition he made two important contacts in an important state. One, Robert Williams, would continue to work to save the plume birds from extinction. He would later join the staff of the United States Biological Survey. The other, the powerful Senator W. Hunt Harris, would betray Dutcher and the new law three years later.

The 1901 law was a stride forward, but it bypassed one essential area—law enforcement. It made no provision for hiring or paying the man who would face the most elemental challenge of all. The warden would have to explain the new law to his friends and neighbors, many of whom would not agree with it. He would have to tack up posters near the rookeries, hoping that would discourage a few of the plumers. But sooner or later the warden would have to confront, face to face, a plume hunter caught in the act at the scene of a crime. And that plume hunter would necessarily be holding a gun in his hands.

Fortunately for Dutcher, money had just become available for manpower. A successful wildlife painter named Abbott Thayer had established a fund to pay wardens. Since Thayer's well-moneyed clients were already lovers of wildlife, he found a fertile area for fund raising within his immediate contacts.

Thayer's bounty solved one problem for Dutcher. His next task would be finding the right man for the Florida job. On his trip to Tallahassee he had set foot on the state's sandy soil but he had not tramped through the sawgrass of the Everglades, struggled to find his way through bewildering mangrove islands, or swatted at swarms of mosquitoes while keeping his eyes alert for Florida's deadly cottonmouth moccasins. He knew nothing about the hunters who had killed the birds legally for decades but now, with a stroke of the governor's pen, would be breaking the law. Since he actually knew nothing firsthand about the territory or its people, he made the only decision available to an intelligent executive.

Dutcher wrote Mrs. Kingsmill Marrs, chairman of the executive committee of the Florida Audubon Society, for help. The likes of Teddy Roosevelt and Grover Cleveland were good to have on your side, but for this particular task, thought Mrs. Marrs, the society would be best served by calling on the expertise of a man whose work had carried him into the wildest reaches of the South Florida wilderness. She called on Kirk Munroe.

Munroe's letter to Mrs. Marrs was promptly forwarded to the chairman. It was followed without delay by a letter from Dutcher to Flamingo, offering the job of Monroe County warden to Guy Bradley.

14 The Badge

JUST NINE DAYS AFTER Dutcher mailed his job offer to the post office in Flamingo, Guy Bradley's reply was on its way to New York. It was a happy moment for Guy. Ahead lay a steady income of thirty-five dollars a month and a chance at last to enter law enforcement. With a wife and child to support, he needed the extra money. And with his appointment as a Monroe County game warden and deputy sheriff, he would finally have earned the right to wear the badge.

Law enforcement was a strong Bradley tradition, but Guy knew the Everglades had little in common with the Chicago streets his relatives patrolled. Danger could lurk behind dense mangroves or deep within the sawgrass. His territory was home to alligators, crocodiles, rattlesnakes, cottonmouth moccasins, and panthers.

Even more dangerous would be the plume hunter. It was a breed he knew. The hunters ranged from kids who shot birds near their homes for a little spending money to rough, hardened, dangerous backwoodsmen who would venture deep into the Florida wilderness to find whatever birds still survived and destroy their rookery, leaving it a wasteland. These men would not go quietly if caught in the act.

One of the most reviled of the plume hunters was Fred Whiting, partly because of his relentless destruction of the many rookeries that had once graced the shores of Lake Okeechobee and partly because of his irritating blasphemy. According to Lawrence E. Will, the Cracker Historian, Whiting was inclined to boast that he feared neither God nor man. Will wrote that "when a squall would hit, the big showoff would shake his fist at the sky, curse the Almighty to his face and dare him to do something about it. . . . But Fred Whiting just blasphemed. One night when a squall came up, he went out doors to secure his boat. A bolt of lighting struck him down there on the beach, which the lake folks knew was a retribution long postponed."[1]

Guy did not expect help from lightning strikes.

In his haste to reply to Dutcher, Guy had been overly brief in answering some of the New Yorker's questions. Dutcher wrote back:

> I do not exactly understand your letter as it seems somewhat contradictory. You state the plume season is from Jan. 1 to June 1, during which time you will need an assistant. Am I to understand from this, as June 1 is so near at hand, that you will not need an assistant at the present time?
>
> You state that you can "get an assistant for $25 for five months." Am I to understand from this that you will have to pay him $5 a month wages?
>
> Am I to understand from your letter that all plume hunting and all shooting of every character of birds stops about June 1?

Guy must have been somewhat dismayed by the chilly tone of the letter's opening comments. Any qualms he may have felt would have been quickly dispelled by the next paragraph from Dutcher:

> While our society has not much money to spend on bird protection and as we have to care for a great many parts of the country, yet I feel we can engage you temporarily at least, and therefore you may consider yourself engaged at $35 per month until further notice. . . . you may consider that your salary will commence on the date that you receive this letter.

Dutcher advised him to visit Key West to secure an appointment as both game warden and deputy sheriff, which would give him the authority to make arrests. He also asked Guy to let him know immediately the names of any New York firms that were buying plumes from Florida and the identity of any traders who were sending feathers to New York, Boston, Philadelphia, or Chicago. If Guy learned of any shipments of plumes leaving Key West, Dutcher asked that he telegraph him immediately to let him know the boat they were on, the express company that was shipping them, and the company they were being sent to. He further requested the names and addresses of every plume hunter in Monroe County and the names of the firms they dealt with.

Headquarters had given Bradley a daunting list of tasks, but he wasted no time in getting back to Dutcher. He cleared up the confusion about his assistant by stating that he had hoped he would be paid not $5 but $25 a month. He explained that the plume hunting season ran from January 15 to April 15:

> That is the nesting season for all the Herons and Ibis and during that time it would be advisable to have an assistant warden for there are some pretty lawless men in the plume hunting business, but from April 15 to Jan. 15 there is of course no plume hunting for the reason that the birds have no plumes....
>
> All shooting doesn't stop after plume season is out, but there is only a little "pot" hunting done such as curlew (White Ibis) and Wood Ibis, Cormorants and other birds that are used for food by some people. The White and Roseate Ibis or Spoonbill are good eating and are hunted the year round, in fact there is a great deal of shooting down here as there is in all sections where the Game laws are not enforced.

Guy Bradley then delivered the only surviving written statement of his plume trade credo:

> I will certainly do all that I can to find out who are the N.Y. buyers. I believe Sterns Bros. are still in the business. They used to buy heavily some years ago when I used to hunt plume birds, but since the Game laws were passed I have not killed a plume bird for it is a cruel and hard calling notwithstanding being unlawful. I make this statement upon honor and can give you as reference a member of your own society, Mr. Kirk Munroe, whom I have known for years.

Guy also acquainted Dutcher with the type of people he knew he would be pitted against in enforcing the bird protection laws:

> I cannot give you the names of hunters in this section for everyone who hunts plumes does so secretly, although I believe all the hunters in this country are not employed by feather firms. There are a good many people in this place but they are all farmers. The hunters are a roving set who live around and in the Ten Thousand Islands on the West Coast of Florida. They often come into our neighborhood and hunt, many of them come from other counties.
>
> It would be necessary for a warden to hunt these people and hunt carefully for he must see them first, for his own sake.

As a skilled boatman, Guy knew his way around the bewildering maze called the Ten Thousand Islands. Most were small mangrove islands, surrounded by such waterways as Lostmans River, the Shark River, and the Chatham River, which flowed out of Chevelier Bay, named after the Old Frenchman.

One of the most notorious characters in the islands was Ed Watson, who lived on the river at Chatham Bend. Watson enjoyed spectacular success in growing vegetables and sugarcane for Key West and New York markets. His cane syrup, Island Pride, was the best in Southwest Florida. But it wasn't his agricultural skill that earned him his status as a violent, ruthless frontier legend. It was whispered that he had killed as many as fifty men and women, among them Belle Starr, the famous woman outlaw who lived in the Oklahoma Territory. Not a man to trifle with.[2]

Part of his sizable income came, it was rumored, from plume hunting, some of it in Bradley's territory. Guy was on good terms with him, which probably meant he knew better than to try to arrest a man as rich, as powerful, and as violent as Watson.

Like Watson, the islands had acquired a fearsome reputation. A writer for London's *Blackwood's Magazine* made some incredible claims. He wrote that a Scotsman, his wife and two daughters, and an Englishman were shipwrecked there early in the eighteenth century. Their descendants lived on the largest of the islands "as a tribe of giant white men, whose minds are the dwarfed minds of six-year-old children. . . . I believe that the females of this idiot colony are practically the only women in this queer corner of the world."

He wrote that so many lawmen had been killed there that sheriffs and deputies would no longer venture onto the island and serve warrants on islanders. Their code of conduct was defined by seven unwritten laws:[3]

Suspect every man.
Ask no questions.
Settle your own quarrels.
Never steal from an islander.
Stick by him, even if you do not know him.
Shoot quick, when your secret is in danger.
Cover your kill.

Despite gross exaggerations and false facts, the bizarre account did reflect the danger that Guy knew lurked in the tangled passageways between islands. He was, after all, well aware of the basic threat all wardens face. Any-time a poacher is caught in the act, the warden must confront an excited, threatened man with a gun in his hand.

On May 29, 1902, Dutcher sent Guy a letter of certification that stated: "Mr. Guy Bradley of Flamingo, Florida, is now employed by the AOU as a warden for the purpose of enforcing the bird law of the State of Florida, Chapter 4957, approved May 29, 1901. . . . The duties of the said Guy M. Bradley are to strictly enforce the said Florida bird law to the effect that he shall prevent the killing of all protected birds or taking their eggs."[4]

Dutcher's letter of certification sent the new bird warden off on what was from the start a wild-goose chase. Guy sailed the *Pearl* over to Key West, where he called on Sheriff Richard Hicks. The sheriff, happy to have another deputy sheriff who could patrol the Cape Sable area for him, took him to the Clerk of the Court, one George W. Reynolds.

The clerk, a native of Austria who had held the post for a decade, refused to swear Guy in because, he contended, the bird law prescribed no penalties for anyone found guilty. Guy visited a lawyer, probably Louis Harris, a Key West attorney who became a good friend. Guy wrote Dutcher telling him that the lawyer believed the dispute could be settled within a few days. One purpose of his letter was "to let you know how hard it is to get these people to understand that there really is a law that protects birds in Florida."

The civilized Dutcher, sputtering incredulously after reading Guy's letter, answered without delay, pointing out that Section 3 of the 1901 law very clearly spelled out the penalties for breaking the law. He threatened to take the matter to the Florida Secretary of State.

Fortunately, Bradley's lawyer bypassed the baleful clerk and had him sworn in by a friendly justice of the peace. The now official deputy sheriff, however, continued in his low opinion of Reynolds, who, he wrote Dutcher, "deserves to be overhauled for he thinks he was Monroe County."

Guy kept busy in his first month as warden. He sailed some seventy-five miles up the west coast to Chokoloskee Island and understandably had trouble with the spelling.

"I have just returned from Chocolus Key," he wrote Dutcher. "There are two stores in that place and they are like all such stores in this part of the state, buyers of Alligator Hides, 'coon' skins and I am almost certain Plumes.

. . . I started at once to do all that I could by informing all the people in this place that the birds protected by law must not be killed and that I had this appointment of Warden. . . . it is gratifying to me to see that a great many people are willing to abide by the law and even help me enforce it if they can."

Bradley also sent Dutcher "the first piece of evidence I have been able to get my hands on." It was a letter or advertising circular from one of the New York firms. A few months earlier, before Guy knew he would be appointed warden, his father, the postmaster, had received a similar circular quoting prices for plumes, but had thrown it away.

Bradley was still a bit in awe of the powerful New Yorker to whom he reported. "I hope," he wrote, "it will be of some good to the cause and if such letters are any service to you I would like to be allowed to make a suggestion, namely that before acting on this letter or circular that I be given a little time to get more of them for you, before putting such firms on their guard. If you could get me the names of other firms that deal in feathers I could get them to send price lists such as the one I have. I only make this suggestion and hope you will not think it too forward or cheeky."

Guy also asked for the right to take some of his minor cases to Howell Cobb Lowe, a justice of the peace who lived near Flamingo, rather than to the county courthouse in Key West. This, he wrote, would save time, since his sailboat was not a particularly swift way to travel to Key West. In addition, it would save money, since the county reimbursed him for mileage expenses. Guy had checked with two sources on the issue. A lawyer told him his cases had to be heard at the county courthouse, while Sheriff Hicks said a justice of the peace would be adequate in some cases. Guy's note to Dutcher closed on a plaintive note:

"I am sorry to appear so ignorant, but I am anxious to do right and not get into trouble."

Dutcher came back with a common-sense answer. One or two birds, justice of the peace. Large number of birds, criminal court in Key West.

The Audubon chairman sent Bradley the names and addresses of seven New York firms he believed were dealing in illegal plumes. He asked Guy to write each of them and ask if they would buy plumes from him and, if so, what kinds of birds they were interested in, how many plumes they would take, and what they would pay.

Guy was lucky he was hired in the off-season. He had until winter to plan and think through how he would approach his new job. Educating his backwoods clientele would probably be his single most productive task. He would have to talk to the Seminoles and Miccosukees, although their plume hunting was seldom excessive. He would have to travel throughout his territory and alert hunters that a new age had dawned. Some would cease shooting plume birds simply because it was now against the law, others because they preferred not to risk arrest, fines, and possible jail time. And, of course, the hard-core few would continue to harvest the birds for the market just as though nothing had changed.

Bradley knew the ways and the tricks of the plumers, the birds, and the market. Flamingos and roseate spoonbills with their glorious pink feathers had once been popular, but their colors tended to fade. Two members of the heron family, however, continued to grow in value as the number of birds plummeted. These were the birds Guy would have to protect, the great white egret, standing more than three feet tall in the marshy waters of the Everglades, and the exquisite snowy egret, the "heron with the golden slippers." Little Snowy stood roughly two feet tall. Clothed in totally white feathers, these egrets massed in a rookery became to the lucky viewer a vision of white clouds in constant motion—and noisy with squawks as raucous as their plumes were beautiful. It would be Guy Bradley's job to save these birds from threatened extinction.

A task Bradley dreaded was telling Captain Smith that the cormorant shooting on Oyster Keys would have to stop. Smith did not take it well. He regarded Oyster Keys as his domain.

On October 13 Guy wrote Dutcher: "The Mosquitoes have been so plentiful this summer that hunters here have not been very numerous in this section, but I expect to have plenty to do pretty soon for Winter is coming on and there will be plenty of Sportsmen shooting at everything they see."

The chairman's ears perked up at the information that his warden would have to contend not just with rough backwoods plume hunters but also with wealthy visitors from the north. He urged Guy to move against any "person who is breaking the law by shooting a protected bird. He should be arrested and fined at once whether he be a rich or poor man, it makes no difference."

Dutcher was particularly anxious for Guy to take action against people who shot wildlife from tour boats, a nasty practice that had been popular in Florida for more than twenty-five years. He wrote:

"Later in the season I intend to have you take a trip on one of the boats that carry tourists as I understand a great many people, while sailing on these small steamboats shoot from the deck at birds on the water and in trees on the banks; of course they cannot pick up the birds but they want to kill them and break the law. . . . Please let me know whether there are any of these small passenger steamers in your locality."

In December Dutcher wrote again, advising Bradley that attorney Robert W. Williams Jr. of Tallahassee, the AOU's counsel in Florida, would be available if Guy had any legal questions on bird protection. He also requested that Guy begin sending him monthly reports, starting in January 1903. The world of paperwork had arrived in Flamingo.

15 On the Job

ON THE LAST DAY OF January, 1903, Guy Bradley pored over his notes. Before him lay the task of writing his first monthly report to Dutcher. He had posted warning notices at Cuthbert Rookery and at feeding grounds for flamingos, herons, and egrets. He had visited people in their homes "far from the main settled district" to talk to them about violations of the law in their area. He had gone to Sandy Key and East Cape Sable. He had traveled deep into the Everglades to the most remote rookeries. He had gone to Alligator Lake, a nesting site so large it now hosted more birds than Cuthbert, the celebrity rookery.

His entry for January 16 read: "Went out to see what someone was shooting and found some hunters shooting alligators for their skins."

Cautiously he had maneuvered in close to the sounds of gunfire, always aware it was best not to barge in blindly when men had guns in their hands. What he found was a group of men hunting legally, for alligators. Still, he knew, it was wise to check them out, since plumers sometimes used legal gator hunting as a cover for killing plume birds illegally.

Jan. 24–25—Visited Alligator Lake and its rookery. Found Wood Ibises getting ready to lay, also plenty of Egrets feeding in the marsh. Narrowly escaped being bitten by a large Cotton-mouthed Moccasin.

"Jan. 26–27—Visited Sandy Key and East Cape Sable, also Egret and duck feeding grounds. Found signs of hunters but no one there, posted warning notices.

"Jan. 29—Heard a lot of shooting out in the Bay, went out in a small boat and tried to catch a boat that was leaving one of the Cormorant Rookeries but the wind sprang up and they got away.

Bradley's report gave no inkling of dangerous tensions building in Cape Sable country. On January 30 Guy's father stepped down as postmaster of Flamingo, a post he had held for nearly three years. He was succeeded by Dan Brinson, Walter Smith's brother-in-law. Brinson held the job for only a brief time before Edwin Bradley took over again on June 25.

Behind the simple chronology of who was going to deliver the mail—and collect a modest salary from Uncle Sam—lay a family quarrel fast coming to a boil.[1] Each of the Bradleys occupied roughly a quarter of a mile of Mingo waterfront. The westernmost part of their holdings was owned by Maggie and Bill Burton. The Burtons' land was bordered on the west by Captain Smith's claim. Beyond that lay Dan Brinson's property.

Burton suspected Smith had encroached on his land. He engaged a surveyor to mark off the lines of his property, originally staked out in the late 1890s when the Smiths and Bradleys settled in Flamingo. The survey indicated Smith had indeed trespassed on the Burtons' land. And who was the town's surveyor? Guy Bradley.

Burton hired a lawyer and brought Smith to court in Key West. He won the case, and with it the undying enmity of the old Confederate sharpshooter. And since Guy had openly backed his brother-in-law, that same fierce antagonism now began to reach out toward him.

At times the feud became childish. Burton, under oath, testified about a blowup with Smith at Harbor Key. Smith, he said, had "carried over supplies for us to Cape Sable and kept them without letting us know, and refusing to sell us groceries when he had ours in his house. On this day we were anchored and he came to us, anchoring near us and Mr. [Robert] Douthit and a man named Greggs asked if we would give them something to eat and I took a small boat and went after them to bring them aboard our boat to give them dinner, and Mr. Douthit proposed that I bring Captain Smith, and I refused to take him aboard my boat to feed him. That is all of it, except a cussing match."

While Brinson was postmaster, Smith had Burton arrested on a charge of unlawfully opening the mails. Nothing came of the charge. Shortly after, Brinson stepped down and the new postmaster, E. R. Bradley, hired his son-in-law to operate the mail boat between Mingo and Key West.

Burton was not the only person Smith was quarreling with. By the time the eventful year 1903 was over, he was fighting with most of the village. His frequent trips to Key West aboard his schooner *Cleveland* gave him ample opportunity to develop strong political contacts in the Monroe County seat. He began exploring with county leaders the possibility of establishing a school in Flamingo. He was concerned because he still had four children of school age. His oldest, Tom, at sixteen was considered too old for schooling. Smith's contacts told him the settlement needed two things—a schoolhouse and a teacher.

Fortunately, the Mingo settlers had already built a small building to serve as a community schoolhouse, meeting place, and church. The single room was about twenty-four by thirty-six feet, big enough to accommodate a dozen children. Not so fortunately, Mingo had been unable to attract either a preacher or a teacher. Occasionally roving missionaries from fundamentalist Protestant sects showed up and blistered Mingo's sinners with visions of hellfire and damnation. Preachers could come and go after a Sunday in the pulpit. A teacher would have to stay with the children day after day.

Smith had a teacher in mind, one Mabel Maloney. She was the daughter of Walter C. Maloney Jr. and the granddaughter of Colonel W. C. Maloney, who had delivered the principal address when Key West observed the nation's centennial on July 4, 1876. The colonel later expanded his remarks into the first published history of the city, *A Sketch of the History of Key West, Florida.*

The old sharpshooter had gone directly to the power structure of Monroe County, even to the point of choosing a teacher with mighty political bloodlines. Unhappily for him and his teacher, strong opposition to her was already building back in Mingo.

Uncle Steve Roberts had little interest in the political scene in Key West. His goal was simply to become the power structure in the narrow corner of the world in which he lived. Both the Smith and the Roberts factions wanted a school in Mingo. The problem was that the two leaders each wanted to do it his way.

"A gathering of neighbors" was the way a young farmer named E. A. McElroy later described a group formed by Uncle Steve to confront Captain Smith. Other descriptions were less kind. Some called it a vigilante committee. McElroy drew the unenviable task of reading to Smith a document drawn up by the "neighbors."

"The gathering was called to ask him to not interfere with us in getting a school," McElroy said. "We were trying to get a school and he was working against us because we objected to the teacher he wanted. And we was appointed to go up and read this paper asking him to attend to his own affairs and not bother us in our endeavors."

One other account said Smith was simply told: "Mind your own business or get out of town."

Smith had looked down the barrels of Union guns. He was not about to back away from a battle with a scrawny little "cattle rustler" like Steve Roberts. At least that was what he was calling him in the story he was spreading about Uncle Steve. Smith said the Roberts clan's departure from Orange County had not been dictated by Dora's health. It was his own skin he was saving, said the captain, a skin in mortal danger from powerful ranchers near Orlando who frowned on cattle rustlers.

Captain Smith won the battle. Mabel Maloney was selected as the teacher for Flamingo's children. Mabel, who stayed at the Smith home, taught primer. She lasted for two terms, a remarkably durable performance. No teacher stayed very long.

"Teachers would come in here for a while, and after a month they would think of something they needed over in Key West or something they forgot and left over there," Mrs. Loren Roberts, Uncle Steve's daughter-in-law, once said. "They'd take the mail boat over to Key West and we'd never see them again."

The schoolhouse became the scene of a bizarre event.

"A School had been established by some obscure kind of connivance between the government and the settlers, but had ignominiously foundered on the rock of prejudice," wrote Vincent Gilpin in his *Cruise of the Seminole,* based on the journal he kept during a South Florida cruise in 1905. "The young men who had built the schoolhouse claimed the right to use it as they pleased out of school hours, and wanted to have a dance. It seemed a commendably cheerful effort in their somber lives, but the schoolmistress did not believe in dancing, and locked them out. They broke in and danced, and she had every man arrested— all thirteen of them—and hauled to Key West to answer for trespass on government property."

All thirteen, including fiddler Guy Bradley, were acquitted; "when they came home from their little excursion in triumph, the chagrined teacher decamped, and as yet no successor has been found," wrote Gilpin. He further noted that the residents of Flamingo "seemed to have strange difficulties in pursuit of both learning and pleasure."

A furious Smith blamed Burton, contributing to the accelerating antagonism between Smith and the Bradley family. Yet in spite of the poisonous atmosphere, Mrs. Bradley and Mrs. Smith, two music lovers, remained close friends.

Against building tensions Guy struggled to keep an increasingly complicated world under control. The winter and spring of '03 saw his first plume hunting season as warden. Fortunately he had the backup services of Bill Burton as his deputy. In the following years he would also make use of the wilderness skills of his brother, Lou, and his two closest friends, Loren and Gene Roberts.

Guy's life was further complicated by important visitors from far away. One, Henry Flagler himself, slipped in unannounced and out again with as little fanfare as possible. What was the tycoon up to? the Mingo settlers wondered. What must he have thought of their strange, scattered collection of fishing shacks perched on stilts? Whatever his reaction, he made no effort to halt the work already under way by the Florida East Coast Railway's engineering department.

The second visitor, William Krome, a muscular young giant who served as assistant engineer for the railroad, was out in the field, continuing his survey of the Cape Sable area when Flagler came and went. On Krome's findings Flagler would base what would be a life-or-death decision for Flamingo. Would it be feasible to extend the railroad to Mingo? Would the Krome report transform mosquito heaven into a bustling seaport town, a West Palm Beach or even a Miami? Would the value of their land, the Bradleys wondered, climb out of sight?

Or would Krome report that the Everglades would suck Flagler's rails and locomotives down into the depths of its black muck? Would he recommend that the rails stretch down through the Keys to Key West, bypassing Flamingo and dooming it to a continued nightmare of poverty, heat, and insects?

Krome spent a great deal of time with the Bradleys. He had attended the University of Illinois before transferring to Cornell to study engineering.

Krome and E.R. Bradley reminisced about their lives in Illinois, but mostly they concentrated on the task at hand. In May Krome wrote to E. Ben Carter, general roadmaster of the railroad at company headquarters in St. Augustine, informing him he had engaged the surveying services of Guy for "a few days field work."

That April two prominent bird protectionists showed up, Arthur Cleveland Bent and the Reverend Herbert Keightly Job, staunch members of the American Ornithologists' Union. Both were well-known authors who would carry their findings back to the scientific community through scholarly journals and books and through meeting with other scientists. They were, however, to report on more than the birds of Cape Sable. Dutcher had also asked them for firsthand accounts of the job being done by the warden of Monroe County, one Guy Bradley.[2]

Job, a Unitarian minister, was anxious to photograph the egrets, herons, and ibis before the poachers destroyed the last of the plume birds. With his bulky camera and his glass plates he accompanied Bradley to a remote lake at East Cape Sable. He wrote:

> There was no boat in the lonely lake, but Bradley proposed to carry a canvas canoe. This we found hidden in the confines of the swamp. It weighed over fifty pounds, and as we pushed on hour after hour through the maze of mangrove roots and tropical jungle, following a trail so blind that we often lost it, I was amazed at the strength of the hardy pioneer who carried it—a man of only moderate weight and size. We took an occasional rest, during one of which Bradley climbed to the nest of a red-shouldered hawk in a slender tree. He brought the young hawk to me to photograph and returned it to its home.

From the mangroves they struggled on into impassable sawgrass, sharp-edged and painful to the touch. Bradley burned it off, and the pair tramped on through the smoke of the grass fire. Along the way, an unrelenting thirst overwhelmed Job. He drank the only water the Everglades could offer him, the brackish swamp water that lay around them in every direction.

Reverend Job had dreamed of being the first ornithologist to make his way to Cuthbert Rookery. It was not to be. The nectar of the swamp was his undoing. The heady brown brew, heavily laced with tannic acid, minerals, and rich decaying tropical vegetation, proved too much for his civilized constitution. On May 1, 1903, Job lay in his bed, his stomach churning beyond his control.

The first ornithologist Bradley led to Cuthbert was Bent, who later described his historic visit in his book *Life Histories of North American Marsh Birds:*

> We had toiled all day, dragging our skiffs over miles of mud flats, poling them through the tortuous channels of sluggish streams, choked with roots and fallen tree trunks, in the almost impenetrable mangrove swamps of extreme southern Florida. The afternoon was well spent when we emerged on the open waters of Cuthbert Lake and saw ahead of us the object of our search, a mangrove island about a mile distant, literally covered with birds. It was a beautiful sight as the afternoon sun shone full upon it; hundreds of white and blue herons, and a score or two of beautiful "pink curlew" could be plainly seen against the dark green of the mangroves, like feathered gems on a cushion of green velvet.
>
> As we drew nearer the picture became more animated, we could see the birds more clearly and we began to realize what a variety of birds and what a host of them the far-famed Cuthbert rookery contained.

Bent estimated that the taller trees in the island's center held three to four hundred American egrets. On the mangroves below them were hundreds of white ibis, some seventy-five to one hundred roseate spoonbills, and along the edges of the islands vast numbers of cormorants, anhingas, and Louisiana and little blue herons.

Guy's account of the trip to Cuthbert Rookery was both shorter and more matter-of-fact:

> May 19—Started up "Snake Creek" and reached Cuthbert Rookery about 9.30. Found Cormorants, Little Blue Herons, Egrets, Louisiana Herons, Snake Birds [anhingas], Rosiate Spoonbills, White Ibises, Wood Ibises and Green Herons nesting and roosting there. Wood Ibises were only roosting, others were nesting.
>
> May 29—After taking a last look at the Rookery we started for Flamingo which we reached at 9 o'clock that night.
>
> May 39—Being Sunday, we went to church.

In his book *Wild Wings,* Reverend Job described the church: "One Sunday I attended a religious service in a building used as chapel and schoolhouse. The women wheeled the children there in baby-carriages, under each of which was tied a smudge-pot. So the carriage rolled along, enveloped in smoke and an outlying cloud of 'skeets' and flies. In the building smudges were going all the time, while the congregation slapped 'skeets' and the children chased horse-flies."

By Monday Job was ready to join the group for a trip to Saw's Lake, where they observed many ibis, pelicans, herons, and a variety of shorebirds. On Wednesday Bradley and Job sailed Guy's small sailboat across Florida Bay to Key Largo to meet Bill Burton, returning from Miami aboard the *Pearl.*

The two boats sailed across the bay to Eagle Key just southeast of Little Madeira Bay. There they found a large concentration of shorebirds. Since Eagle Key was in Dade County, Guy was serving not as a county warden but rather as a tour guide for a naturalist fascinated by his first visit to the mangrove wilderness. He and Job started back to Flamingo in Guy's small boat. Heavy winds forced Guy to find a safe harbor. Job used the time well. A skilled photographer, he busied himself taking pictures of shorebirds. On Sunday, May 10, there was no stopping to go to church. The reverend kept taking pictures.

At 10 P.M. Sunday they reached Porpoise Point and camped there for the night on Guy's boat. The next day was the one Job had been waiting for. They arrived at Flamingo at about eleven o'clock and started for Cuthbert Rookery the same day.

The first stage of their journey was made in Guy's small, open sailboat with a flat-bottomed skiff in tow. That night they slept under a tent set up on the boat, anchored near a small bay called Snake Bight. Job did not sleep well. Storm clouds hid the moon, and the darkness around them was a dense black. The sounds of the night did little to relax him—the scream of a panther off in the jungle, the angry hum of mosquitoes, and the constant pelting of a spring rain. There was no relief for Job. When the rain slackened, the mosquitoes just became more aggressive.

The reverend was not unhappy when Guy roused him at dawn from his unsatisfying slumber. This day Job would finally make it to Cuthbert. With luck. The problem was the rain. Finally it slowed, and the clouds began to break.

"I think we can make it now," said Guy.

He anchored their boat near the shore, probably in Snake Bight. They packed blankets and provisions in the small skiff and moved toward the mass of mangroves.

"No opening whatsoever was visible," wrote Job, "but, on pulling apart the branches with our hands, we could see a narrow stream of water flowing into the sea. The branches closed behind us, and we were in the meshes of the mangrove swamp. The channel was just wide enough to float the skiff. Branches met overhead and shut out the sunlight; tangled roots and snags reached everywhere through the water, across which trunks and limbs had grown or fallen. Some of these had been chopped out previously by the guide, so our task was easier."

The two of them sculled and paddled, poled and dragged the boat for seven miles over and under obstructions. Once, Job stepped into a gator hole and knew the sudden terror of sinking into the brown water. Bradley pulled him out. Before the adventure was over, Job had paid Guy back by helping him out of another hole the gators had dug. Occasionally they enjoyed a respite in crossing a small, unobstructed lake before the next overgrown channel.

Then their skiff emerged into Cuthbert Lake. The patience of Job had at last been rewarded.

"There lay the famous island," wrote Job, "not altogether white with birds, yet enough of them in evidence to verify the wonderful tales I had heard. . . . we were well-nigh exhausted when we glided into the lovely lake and reached the island known as Cuthbert Rookery, with its thousands of breeding ibises, herons, egrets, spoonbills, flamingoes and cormorants."

For a photographer-naturalist like Job the rookery was a feast. For two and a half days he took pictures, some from the boat, some like his close-up of young spoonbills in their nest from the island itself. He was particularly proud of a photo he took that occupied a full page of his book *Wild Wings*. Its caption read: "Ibises and cormorants leaving the rookery. 'My first picture.'"

In addition to his photographs, Reverend Job took extensive notes. To him, visiting Cuthbert was the experience of a lifetime.

"Well, how would you like to try this alone?" Guy asked him, then continued, "I come in here two or three times each season, first to post warning notices, and then to see if the birds are doing well. And whether any plume hunters are killing them."

On May 14 Bradley and Job started back. Weary from their labors, they rested on the fifteenth, then moved on again the next day, a Saturday. This time they visited the large, bustling rookery at Alligator Lake.

Bradley reported: "Found White Ibises, Snowy Herons, Rosiate Spoonbills, Egrets and Snake Birds nesting, all have young. Also saw Wood Ibis feeding about in the swamp."

While Bradley and Job were at Cuthbert, plume hunters had come by the Flamingo area. Following up a tip, Guy uncovered news of the deterrent value of a warden: "Found out that the hunters had gone on when they found out there was a Game Warden near them, and as they went into Dade County I did not follow them for they cannot do any damage in Dade County." By this time the area near Miami held no concentrations of birds worth a warden's or a plume hunter's time.

Three days after his return from Alligator Lake with Job, Bradley saw a disturbing sight—smoke rising from the woods near the lake. He went back to Alligator Lake to see who was burning the woods. What he found was a party of Krome's surveyors. Three days later he went back to the lake again, just to be extra careful.

"Went out near Alligator Lake watching the surveyors to see that they did not shoot birds," he noted in his report to Dutcher. Guy had reason to be suspicious. Once, on a surveying job with Charlie Pierce, he too had done a little plume hunting on the side.

16 A Boat Named *Audubon*

WHEN GOTTLOB KROEGEL arrived at Barker's Bluff in 1881, he knew he had found an ideal homestead.[1] He had come to America from the hilly country around Chemnitz, Germany, and now in the otherwise flat country just south of Cape Canaveral he had discovered the only high ground in the lands along the tidewater lagoon called Indian River. From the bluff he and his immigrant family could gaze across at a cluster of mangrove islands populated by a rich variety of birds, particularly the lively, noisy brown birds that gave the largest the name Pelican Island. In the forests to the west lived Florida panther, wildcats, and bears, and in the Sebastian River flowing into the lagoon he would of course find alligators, and in all the waterways nearby a plentiful supply of both fresh- and saltwater fish.

The bluff had not been created by the forces of nature. It was instead an ancient Indian shell mound, dating back to the days when the Ais Indians roamed the area. The mound was "higher than the tallest cabbage palms, as large as a football field." It took its name from its first settler, a Mr. Barker, who was reportedly killed by Seminole Indians angered when they learned that the whiskey he had been selling them was watered down. At first the location did not prove a lucky one for the Kroegels, either. Two years after they made their home on the bluff, a hurricane blew their first modest dwelling away.

For young Paul Kroegel, seventeen when the family came to the Indian River, the location was enchanting from the start. He loved to look across the lagoon at the busy flocks of birds at the rookery on Pelican Island, which was owned by the federal government. By the late 1890s Paul no longer liked what he saw. Boaters on the Indian River, which stretched from Titusville to Jupiter, armed themselves with rifles and gunned down the pelicans as they cruised past the government-owned island. The dying birds, of course, fluttered down into the tidal waters and promptly were forgotten as the boats cruised by. Plume hunters, though less of a threat to the pelicans, also wreaked damage on the egrets and herons on the island.

Kroegel found kindred spirits at nearby Ma Latham's Oak Lodge. Located on a point of land near Micco, a village just north of his home in the little settlement now called Sebastian, Ma Latham's became a favorite of many of America's most influential ornithologists and naturalists, among them Frank Chapman, the Reverend Herbert K. Job, Arthur Cleveland Bent, Abbott Thayer, and John Burroughs. Chapman, whose mother had a house in Gainesville, first came to Oak Lodge on his honeymoon in 1898.[2]

Paul Kroegel talked often with Chapman about the need for an official warden to protect the birds nesting on the government-owned island. In the meantime Paul assumed the duties of a warden, unofficial and unpaid, and continued to press Chapman to use his considerable influence in high places.

Chapman knew the right "high place" to go—President Theodore Roosevelt, already a staunch conservationist. In March 1903 Chapman and other leading ornithologists met with the president to try to persuade him to designate Pelican Island, already government land, as a protected wildlife refuge.

Nothing in the Constitution or in existing law spelled out the power for him to create wildlife refuges, but, being Teddy Roosevelt, the president next asked his advisors if anything said he could not do it. When he learned there were no bars to declaring the island the nation's first wildlife refuge, he said, "Very well, then I so declare it." An executive order signed by President Roosevelt followed on March 14, 1903.

Ten days later Washington sent official notification to Kroegel that he had been appointed "warden in charge of the Pelican Island Reservation, Florida, in the Division of Biological Survey in the United States Department of Agriculture."

Kroegel's dream had come true. Not only was he the official warden of America's first national wildlife refuge, he now would be paid a salary—one dollar a month.

The money, happily, was unimportant to Kroegel except as a symbol. Protecting the birds was to him a labor of love, and he already earned a living from his successful boatbuilding business. In fact, at the time he received his papers from the Department of Agriculture, he had just finished building a boat for Audubon. In his annual report for 1902 Dutcher had recommended the purchase of a powered boat for Guy Bradley, still struggling to cover a vast territory in a small sailboat, subject to the whims of the wind. As always with National Audubon's early projects, funding was a problem. The Florida Audubon Society's executive committee, however, raised three hundred dollars to commission Kroegel to build a seaworthy open launch, twenty-three feet in length, equipped with a three-horsepower engine fueled by naphtha, a highly explosive petroleum product used in the early days of powerboating. The committee, appropriately, named the boat *Audubon*.

On May 24, 1903, the same date as Kroegel's official appointment, a telegram—always an occasion for excitement in Flamingo—reached Guy. With pleasure he read the message from Dutcher, instructing him to sail to Miami, where he would meet Kroegel and pick up the powered naphtha launch.

The two wardens had much in common, although one worked for the government, the other for a private organization. Both had come to Florida from Chicago, where they had lived as children. Both wardens were music lovers who performed at local events, Guy playing the violin, Kroegel the accordion.[3] Both had recently married. Six years older than Bradley, Kroegel, however, had learned the craft of carpentry in Chicago, and it served him well in building boats and in establishing himself in the young community of Sebastian. In 1905 Paul would become the first commissioner of the newly created St. Lucie County and chairman of the county board that voted to build the first bridge across the Sebastian River.[4]

As the official warden for Pelican Island, Kroegel showed considerable independent judgment. When the Department of Agriculture sent him an American flag to post on Pelican Island, he placed it instead atop Barker's Bluff. Boats cruising on Indian River could see it at a considerable distance. Since they customarily tooted their boat horns when they saw the flag, the familiar blast sent a personal signal to the warden to move quickly to the island to discourage any bird shooters.

During Kroegel's first year as warden he reported that the pelicans had deserted the large island and moved to smaller mangrove islands nearby. Chapman suggested that the move had been caused by the decline in trees on Pelican Island. Kroegel concluded the birds had moved out because they were disturbed by a large warning sign posted on the island for the National Committee of Audubon Societies. Kroegel took the sign down. Two days later the birds came back.

Guy Bradley and Paul Kroegel met for the first, and only, time in Miami on May 29. Guy had traveled alone in his small sailboat—a mistake, as it turned out. He reached Miami the night of May 28 and first saw his new boat and his fellow warden the following morning. Not long after that Guy's troubles began.

His first problem arose when he tried to tow his sailboat behind the new launch. He soon found that the *Audubon* lacked the power to handle so heavy a load. "So stopped at Cocoanut Grove and sold my boat," he wrote to Dutcher. "Went back to Miami to get new battery for the one in the *Audubon* is exhausted having run the engine for 24 miles and being a cheap dry battery which cannot stand continued use."

In his June report Guy was critical of Kroegel's handling of the boat during its 240-mile trip to Coconut Grove. He complained that the battery had given out completely because it was run "without any help from Dynamic Auto Sparker or Magneto which it is not made to do for a dry battery will not last with continual use like a wet battery will."

Over the next few months Dutcher read more about the care and feeding of a naphtha launch than he cared to know. Guy, who enjoyed working on boats, spent six days in June trying to get the launch in good operating condition. He was grounded, too, by heavy rains and stormy weather. So much rain fell that Bradley had to buy thirty yards of "No. 8 canvas" in Key West to cover his boat. The heavy summer rains brought other complications. The swamps near the cape became too "full of water" for him to travel through and, even worse, the rains brought a new crop of mosquitoes. On July 16 Guy wrote: "Started to Key West on Schooner *Volusia* having decided to move my family to town, for the mosquitoes and bad weather are too bad on the main land."

The real reason the Bradleys moved to Key West was Fronie's pregnancy. Her second child was expected in the fall. Heat and humidity made the cape an unfit world for an expectant mother. Fronie stayed with "Aunt Fanny" McCook, her best friend, at the McCook home at 926 Pauline's Alley.

In early August Bradley spent more time working on the *Audubon* than he did protecting birds. He cleaned and overhauled the engine, worked on the engine's firing pin, and on August 11 painted the boat's bottom with copper paint. The next day storm signals were flying. In looking for safe harbor Guy ran over a sunken log and bent the propeller "pretty badly." Not until August 22 did he have the engine back in good operating condition, just in time for an extended trip looking for man-o'-war nesting sites. The morning of August 24, 1903, just before he left, he wrote Fronie:

> My Darling Wife:
> I reached Flamingo last Thursday, and have been busy fixing the launch. I hauled her out and lined up the engine and shaft and put a new brass box on the shaft between the engine and the stern bearing and the engine runs nicely now. Will and Maggie, also their boy, are well. Shelly [Fronie's younger brother] is having a good time and has not been homesick at all, he is all right, hasn't had any bad spells at night.
> The old folks are coming home in a little sharpie the Old Gent bought on Lake Worth. I am anxious about you and Morrell and want to come home but I have got to stay away a long time yet I am afraid.

By "afraid" did Guy mean he was sorry he would be away quite a while? Or was he actually fearful of events unfolding at Flamingo? Could it have been an unusual transaction that put a gun in the hands of Walter Smith's oldest son, Tom, whom Bradley had already had to arrest for plume hunting?[5] In the next paragraph of his letter Guy mentions a report about a man described as "crazy" but not dangerous. The man, Fred Hurse, had apparently feared he had "done harm" to Captain Smith "by saying mean things about him." Smith declined to accept five dollars from Hurse, but agreed to let the man give Tom "his Gun and Ammunition."

In his closing paragraph Guy wrote: "Well, I can't think of anything more to say except Kiss Papa's Boy for me and get some one to Kiss yourself for me. Your Loving Boy, Guy."

In September Guy began to put the *Audubon* to good use. He cruised up the west coast through the Ten Thousand Islands. He visited Lostmans River, the Shark River, and the Rogers River. His entry for September 9:

"Saw two canoe loads of Seminole Indians on their way from their camping grounds to the trading stores at Chocoluskey." The trading posts he referred to were McKinney's and Smallwood's.

The next day a sixty-mile-an-hour wind forced him into a safe harbor. The following day it was worse. "Sept. 11th— Hurricane still blowing with heavy rain falling almost all day. The sea birds are almost all coming inland and are either flying very low or roosting on the trees near the river sides. I have seen about two thousand Man-o-War birds and four thousand gulls and terns today."

The following day the storm was past. The cape country escaped the worst of the storm of September 11–13. All told, fourteen deaths and heavy shipping losses were recorded.

Morrell was taken sick in late September. His illness, coupled with the late stages of Fronie's pregnancy, distracted Guy so much that he neglected to write a report for October. Dutcher wrote in November, requesting the missing report. Guy wrote back very briefly, reporting one arrest of a man named Sam Davis in Key West. He also took more pictures with the camera Dutcher had sent him. He shipped photographic plates to the chairman, hoping they were better than earlier ones he had taken.

On November 8 the waiting was finally over for the young couple. Their second child, another boy, was born at the McCook home on Pauline's Alley. They named him Ellis.

The year 1903, Guy's first full year as warden, had been a busy one. That year the price offered to hunters for egret plumes rose to thirty-two dollars an ounce, more than twice the price for an ounce of gold. Four egrets had to die to yield an ounce of plumes. Bradley's vigilance had helped create a scarcity that was driving the price up—and ultimately making the rookeries all the more tempting to plume hunters.

A new baby and a job well done were causes for rejoicing at Guy's home. The year brought no such good news for his father. From working with Krome and his men, E. R. could see that the cape's chances as the railroad terminus were fading. He had lobbied hard for a location close to his holdings, but Krome was not buying his arguments.

In early June a brief item had appeared in the *Miami Metropolis* about Krome and his team of sixteen assistants. The Flamingo correspondent, Justice of the Peace H. C. Lowe, wrote that although the men had been asked by the company not to discuss their work, "It is easy to see that none of them expect to see a very great city at Cape Sable at any early day."

That fall Edwin Bradley learned the bad news officially. Engineering reports told Henry Flagler that the cost of the Cape Sable route would be prohibitive. On the other hand, building the Key West extension across the Keys was feasible.

"Go ahead," said Flagler. "Go to Key West."[6]

Bradley's dream of wealth was shattered. He was now the land agent for land worth next to nothing.

17 Trouble at Cuthbert

"YOU ARE CERTAINLY FORTUNATE in your selection of wardens for the protection of this inaccessible region, and it would be hard to find better men for this work than Messrs. Bradley and Burton."

With satisfaction Dutcher read the report of Bent and Job. In fact, he was so pleased that he had it printed in its entirety in the January 1904 issue of *The Auk,* the journal of the American Ornithologists' Union. It went on to say:

> The rookeries are so widely scattered and traveling is so difficult, either on land or water, that it is almost impossible for two, or even three, men to cover this whole region at all thoroughly. The native conchs and negroes, many of whom are desperate characters, can, by watching the warden's movements visit the rookeries with impunity and make wholesale depredations on the young herons, ibises and even cormorants for food. Several expeditions of this kind have already been broken up by the judicious employment of negro spies, who keep the wardens informed.

Most of the blacks who lived in the Flamingo area were charcoal burners. They lived back from the water, east of Mingo in the wooded patches near the buttonwoods they used to make charcoal for the stoves of Key West. Since the Bradley family schooner was used to carry cargo to Key West, both Guy and Bill Burton probably knew them through the buttonwood trade. Not surprisingly, no mention of informants can be found in any of the surviving reports sent to Dutcher by the warden, described admiringly by Job as "tough as a red mangrove."

Despite their praise for the work of the Monroe County wardens, Bent and Job recognized that attacking the supply side of the plume industry was not the answer.

The most effective work against the plume hunters can be done by working against the purchasers of plumes, thus destroying the demand, rather than against the hunters themselves, who are expert woodsmen and very difficult to catch. All of the principal rookeries and roosts have been thoroughly posted and wherever we went to explore a new one, Bradley always carried a supply of warning notices, which he nailed to trees or stakes in conspicuous places.

The natives are beginning to realize that the birds are to be protected and that the wardens are fearless men who are not to be trifled with. The Bradleys have the reputation of being the best rifle shots in that vicinity and they would not hesitate to shoot when necessary. The Bradleys and Burton together would be more than a match for any party they are likely to meet.

The two ornithologists were particularly impressed with the Alligator Lake Rookery. There egrets, herons, ibis, and spoonbills filled the trees and the skies overhead in numbers so great that Bent and Job, given their tight schedule, found a population estimate impossible.

In Southern Florida, as elsewhere, the plume hunters have done their work thoroughly, but there is not much to be feared from them in future, simply because there are very few desirable plume birds left for them to hunt. The American Egret and Snowy Herons are so reduced in numbers that it does not pay to hunt them. There are, however, a few of these birds still left in nearly all of the less accessible rookeries, so that under adequate protection, they ought to increase sufficiently to partially restock their former haunts.

The scientists were wrong. There was still a great deal to be feared from the plume hunters. Not long after *The Auk* report was published, they struck again.

In the winter of 1904 Guy Bradley received word that another distinguished ornithologist would be visiting him. Intrigued by the report from Bent and Job, Chapman had decided he would like to see Cuthbert Rookery. On March 12, 1904, Bradley wrote to Dutcher about the proposed visit of Chapman and his wife, Fanny. He feared the *Audubon* would not be comfortable enough for them and suggested he meet them with the *Pearl,* "a large and roomy boat," at either Miami or Key West. In the same letter Bradley wrote:

I have been cruising through the Ten Thousand Islands along the west coast of Florida . . . posting warning notices and distributing the leaflets containing the game laws of Florida among the people living in that part of the county. I have met several parties of hunters, but they were only hunting alligators and otters. I visited several rookeries—most of which used to be large egret and heron nesting places, but are almost, if not quite, deserted now. There are not many tourists in this county at present, but I manage to keep an eye upon those whom I find cruising near any of the large rookeries which are situated among the Keys which lie near the Mainland. I have seen a few large launches going by on their way from Punta Gorda to Miami, but as they did not stop in my territory I did not have to watch them very long.

It was a busy time for Bradley. As he visited deserted nesting sites back in the mangroves or in the islands in the Glades, he must have been pleased at the progress he had made. Still, there was always the reality he had to live with. Any day, a successful raid on one of his rookeries could move him back to the scene he faced at the start.

A warning arrived all too quickly. In the winter of 1904 Guy received information from an unexpected source—from Walter Smith. At least, this was the claim made later by the captain, still bristling from his clashes with Steve Roberts.

"Those Robertses are planning a big plume raid," Smith told Guy.

"Yeah? Where?"

"Cuthbert."

Guy's answer, Smith later said, was: "The bird business is my business. You attend to your own God-damned business and leave my business alone."[1]

Shortly thereafter, Cuthbert Rookery was shot out. Two years of hard work by Bradley were obliterated by one devastating raid.

Smith was open in his contempt for Bradley.

"Bradley didn't stop it because he was part of the Roberts gang," Smith charged. "He got a piece of the profits. He got paid off for looking the other way.

"He only enforces the law against the small fry. Uncle Steve and his wild boys are just too much for one bird warden to handle."

Who were the "small fry" Smith spoke of? Did he mean his own son Tom? Smith's seventeen-year-old now had a gun, given to him by the demented Hurse. Tom openly shot birds in violation of the law and at some date in 1904 was arrested by Bradley.

No arrests of Uncle Steve, known to shoot birds of plume when it suited his purpose, show up in the few records that remain from that time. Like Ed Watson, Roberts was a man best left alone.

Long after Bradley's time, an Audubon warden at Flamingo was asked, "Did you ever arrest any of the Robertses?"

"I made that mistake once," he replied. "I saw one of the Roberts boys pull up to the dock with dead plume birds in his boat. I walked out on the dock to arrest him. The next thing I knew I heard an explosion and my glasses flew right off my face. I looked around and there by the dock stood Uncle Steve. He had a gun in his hand, and a smile on his face."[2]

Frank Chapman met Bradley not at Miami or Key West but at Tavernier Creek near Key Largo. The news he received from the warden was all bad. The nesting season, Guy told him, had developed a month earlier than expected; there would be fewer birds to see. Then he told him about Cuthbert.

"Cuthbert Rookery has been shot out," Guy said. "You could've walked right around the rookery on them birds' bodies, between four and five hundred of them."

A stunned Chapman returned to Miami without visiting Flamingo. There he would have encountered the rumors about Guy's role in the raid, which might have affected his report to Dutcher. But, just as Bent and Job had before him, Chapman gave Bradley high marks for his work:

"I was favorably impressed with Bradley, and believe he is doing the best he can. He is somewhat inclined to talk about himself and his work and the risks he runs in the performance of his duties, but he has, I think, a pride in his office and an enmity for law breakers which would lead him to convict them, if possible. He seems especially outraged by the looting of the Cuthbert Rookery and obviously would be glad to get the offenders."

Chapman later wrote: "Under his guardianship the 'white birds' had increased to numbers, which, with aigrettes selling at $32 an ounce, made the venture worth the risk (for there was risk; as the man who attempted to 'shoot out' a rookery while Bradley was on guard would probably have lost his own 'plume'); the warden was watched and in his absence his charges were slaughtered."

Chapman then made a prophetic statement: "That man Bradley is going to be killed sometime. He had been shot at more than once, and some day they are going to get him."

In time Smith's disturbing Cuthbert charges reached Audubon in New York. No records are available of the ensuing probe, but a later Audubon executive recalled that the matter was investigated. The captain's charges were found to be baseless.[3]

So who did shoot out the rookery? Uncle Steve and his boys? Walter Smith and his boys? Or possibly the "roving hunters" from back in the Ten Thousand Islands? Or none of the above?

18 Life in Flamingo

I N F L A M I N G O it is doubtful that everyone was upset by Flagler's decision to bypass the cape. People who had fled to Mingo would not have applauded the coming of law and order. Where else could they go? Deep into the Everglades, the Ten Thousand Islands, the islands in Florida Bay? Or maybe the islands off the coast of British Honduras, now known as Belize? Plume hunters like Gregorio Lopez already knew about Honduras.

Life went on at Cape Sable. The settlers kept struggling to wrest a living from a land poor in opportunity. They still turned to commercial fishing, charcoal burning, trapping of furbearing animals, plume hunting, serving as hunting and fishing guides for wealthy sportsmen from the north, raising vegetables and sugarcane, and distilling a raw whiskey called "low bush lightning" or sometimes "Cape Sable agerdent."

Not all of the raw whiskey was for sale. Men trapped in a hard world often submerged themselves in all-day drinking bouts, turning meaner with each swig from the jug. Then after dark they would sometimes engage in the nasty Flamingo sport of firing their guns at the homes of people they disliked. They aimed high, since their goal was not to hit anyone but rather to scare the daylights out of their enemies. Still, if a tall person happened to be standing at the wrong time in the wrong place, the results could be deadly.

But life was not without its light side.

One day Guy asked his pal Loren Roberts, "How would you like to put on the gloves and box my wife?"

"Don't be silly, Guy,"

"I'm not kidding you, Loren. Fronie can box. Come on over and see for yourself."

"I'd hurt her," said Loren.

"No you won't. She can take care of herself. More likely to hurt you."

Still disbelieving, Loren went to Guy's house. He saw boxing gloves, and there was Fronie, ready to put them on.

Careful not to hurt Fronie, Loren found to his amazement that she needed very little help. A big girl, she defended herself well against the awkward, half-hearted punches that Loren threw. And from time to time she scored with blows that slipped past Loren's untrained defenses.

Guy roared with laughter when Fronie belted Loren. He was very proud of his wife.[1]

The fun-loving Fronie brought an important new element into the life of the overly serious Guy Bradley. But then, he had something to be serious about. His job was a difficult, dangerous one. His responsibilities were enormous, yet his means of meeting them were meager. His territory was just too big. Even with a deputy he could not cover all the vulnerable sites. He could not camp out week after week at Cuthbert Rookery or Alligator Lake. Sooner or later the rookeries would lie unprotected before the rifles of the plumers.

In 1904 his reports to Dutcher became less regular, partly the result, he said, of sickness. Perhaps a part of it was stress.

In the late fall of that year and into the winter of 1905, Bradley made three arrests involving Smith family members for shooting birds illegally. He arrested Captain Smith once and on two occasions brought charges against the captain's oldest son, Tom. The seventeen-year-old was considered an unruly teenager, but in Mingo objections to his bird shooting were mild. "Boys will be boys" was the general reaction. The populace did not really consider bird killing a major offense.

Why did Guy arrest Tom? Since he was quite young, wouldn't a warning and a good talking-to have served better? Guy thought not, because Tom's shooting was open, flagrant, defiant, a clear challenge to his authority. If a mere boy could shoot birds under Guy's nose, his days as a lawman would be over. On the frontier you couldn't back down.

After the second arrest of Tom Smith, the captain's fury exploded: "You ever arrest one of my boys again, I'll kill you."

Guy knew the captain was not bluffing. The warden had been shot at before, and he was well aware of the hazards of his job. But what could he do? Resign his commission and turn in his badge? Just because an old man had threatened him? He would have been disgraced in the eyes of the town and, even worse, in the eyes of his family. Fronie was willing to put on the gloves and stand up to the men. Could Guy do less? Could Morrell and Ellis handle the derisive laughter that would surely follow if their father caved in?

Guy Bradley had no choice. He had been threatened. He had to keep doing his job.

In the winter of 1905 Smith threw another challenge at Bradley. He decided to use his political pull in Key West to oust Guy from his job as Audubon warden and Monroe County deputy sheriff.[2]

"I'd be a better warden," Smith told the county commissioners. "Swear me in as deputy and I'll make sure Cuthbert Rookery is protected."

The captain, however, had not done his homework. He did not realize that the warden was appointed by the governor on Audubon's recommendation. And perhaps even more to the point, he did not know that the warden's pay came through an organization that had now been incorporated as the National Association of Audubon Societies.

And Audubon wanted nothing to do with Walter Smith.

Dutcher decided the time had come to take the train to South Florida. From St. Augustine south he rode the rails of Henry Flagler. He stopped off briefly in Sebastian to visit with Paul Kroegel. In Palm Beach he stayed at the Palm Beach Hotel, where he noted in his journal that hotels, railroads, steamships, everything "belongs to Flagler." Dutcher visited with Charles Cory, a wealthy naturalist, author, golf champion, and playboy, who informed him that Flagler's home, Whitehall, was "the finest private residence in America." In awe of Palm Beach, he called the Royal Poinciana "the largest hotel I ever saw" and described Flagler's new hotel, the Breakers, as "magnificent."[3]

The Audubon chairman was less impressed with Miami. "This town is not much to see. The houses are all very low and flat and quite as tropical as Palm Beach but not so fashionable."

What he enjoyed most on his boat trip from Miami to Key West was the water, sparkling with "the most beautiful colors, some a perfect ultramarine blue, some a cobalt blue, then where the bottom was of coral almost a purple." From the boat he saw sharks, porpoises, and flying fish as well as man-o'-war birds, cormorants, and laughing gulls.

On February 9, Dutcher checked into Key West's finest, the Jefferson Hotel on Duval Street, to await the arrival of Guy Bradley at the helm of the

Audubon. But first he took a taxicab and saw the sights of Key West. He visited the fishing docks and the docks where schooners were berthed, "very small, old and dirty, manned and sometimes captained by Negroes." He noted many Cubans in the town, most of them employed in the thriving cigar industry. The next day, a Friday, he referred to the United States Navy base as "quite a large military station" on the island. Dutcher met with Captain Charles G. Johnson, keeper of the Sand Key Lighthouse and also Audubon bird warden for the small area near the light. He chatted too with John W. Atkins, AOU member and now head of the island's telephone and telegraph company. For the first time he saw sponge and green turtle markets.

After three years of talking to each other through the mails, Dutcher and the Everglades warden finally met on February 11, 1905. "He is a young man rather small but bright," he wrote in his journal.

Together Bradley and Dutcher met with chairman J. R. Curry of the Monroe County commission. The Audubon leader renewed his acquaintance also with Senator Hunt Harris, who had helped him secure passage of the AOU's bird protection law. Amicably they discussed establishing a statewide game commission. From his visit with Key West's most powerful political leader, Dutcher had no inkling of the betrayal Harris would visit upon the Audubon cause before the year was over.

Dutcher apparently presented his case without ruffling the feathers of the Conch commissioners unduly, not an easy task for a Yankee from New York City. After he returned home he wrote to the commission, making the Audubon position very clear.

"I beg to call your attention to the application of Mr. Guy M. Bradley for appointment as county game warden. You recollect that this petition was filed early during the present month by Mr. Bradley and myself and that we also had the privilege of calling upon the chairman of your board. The appointment of Mr. Bradley will be a distinct gain to your county for the reason that our society pays his salary thus relieving the county treasury and we also supply Mr. Bradley a power launch with which to travel throughout the waters of the county."

Dutcher closed with a gently phrased threat: "If he is not appointed in your county it will be necessary for us to transfer him and his boat to some other part of Florida. I should be glad to hear what action your board takes."

The answer came back promptly from Eugene W. Russell, circuit court clerk: "Appointment recommended by board last evening. Governor will probably appoint."

On March 22, 1905, H. Ray Crawford, Florida secretary of state, sent Bradley his official appointment as "Fish and Game Warden in and for Monroe County."

19 Back on the Job

ON MARCH 25, 1905, the Bradleys gazed out across Florida Bay at a large yacht aground at low tide in the shoal waters off Flamingo. Soon a dinghy was on its way to shore bearing three men from the luxury yacht, a sixty-four-foot yawl-rigged sharpie named *Seminole*. The men turned out to be Captain Blackington and two old Palm Beach friends of the Bradley family, Vincent Gilpin and Sanford Cluett. Gilpin, a boater, photographer, and author, kept a log of the cruise, later published as *The Cruise of the Seminole*.[1]

"I took the dinghy ashore to look things up, found Guy Bradley, and had a good talk about old times at Palm Beach," wrote Gilpin. "He was married and settled down as game-warden and sheriff; his father was postmaster, and his brother-in-law, Burton, was mail-carrier from Key West. It was quite a family community, and seemingly a happy one, though a little handicapped, by lack of sufficient fresh water. Their land was most promising in appearance—a deep black soil, and they got good crops of fruits and vegetables, including limes."

In the afternoon Gilpin, his wife, and his son Vincent Jr. called on Edwin and Lydia Bradley, "finding them exactly as we remembered them, fifteen years before, on Lake Worth. Mr. Bradley had taken the post office, he said, because there was no one else in the settlement capable of performing the duties, and more than half the mail coming to the office was addressed to him. He was also Flagler's land-agent, and bitterly disappointed that the Cape Sable route for the Key West railroad had been given up."

At the Bradleys' home Gilpin also noted the number of magazines and books on hand, "evidently as important to the family as ever, stacked high on every hand, and kept in a degree of good order which marked their preciousness. We greatly regretted not having even a few volumes to leave in return for their generosity. . . . It seemed a forbiddingly lonely life for people of their tastes, but Mr. Bradley said they took an occasional holiday in Miami when the mosquitoes got very bad."

Guy provided a tour of the rookeries for Blackington and Cluett and took them fishing for tarpon "without much success" and later for sharks. Cluett proved skilled in spearing sharks until one of them seized his favorite harpoon in its teeth and swam off with it.

Cluett, an old friend of Guy's, was vice president of Cluett, Peabody & Company, a huge textile firm that manufactured a popular product called Arrow shirts. Sanford Cluett captured a measure of immortality for himself by inventing a process to prevent cotton cloth from shrinking. His company showed its appreciation by naming the process Sanforizing.[2]

Emma Gilpin's detailed diary of the trip also contained numerous mentions of the Bradleys. Mrs. Gilpin, in her journal of the cruise, described Lydia Bradley as "looking much as she did." Edwin was grayer, she noted, but as "fond of books and papers as ever." In fact, he gave the yachting party copies of New York papers that were less than two weeks old. The Bradleys, she wrote, had a pair of horses to work the land and raised peaches, limes, lemons, guavas, and bananas.

From Mrs. Gilpin's journal: "March 27, 1905—[Guy] Bradley comes aboard at 8 and points out interesting spot on the map east of here. Tells of his efforts to preserve the birds as game warden—interesting visit to bird island where white and blue herons and other birds are nesting. Photographed them. . . . All are much disappointed that Flagler will not build his R.R. down this way as was first surveyed, hoped to sell their good black-soil garden land at $4000 an acre. Alas for their hopes."[3]

Cluett, who had known him for seventeen years, later observed that Guy seemed worried. "There's a poacher I'm gonna have to arrest," he told Cluett. "He's a dangerous character."

Guy showed him his nickel-plated .32-caliber pistol.

"Altogether inadequate," said Cluett.

When their yacht was ready to return to Palm Beach, Guy rowed out to tell them good-bye, bringing Morrell with him. It would be the last time Cluett saw Guy.

A few weeks later Guy received a magazine in the mail, followed a few days later by a letter from Gilpin. Guy wrote back to him at his home in West Chester, Pennsylvania.[4]

> My Dear Friend,
>
> Your welcome letter reached me a few days ago, sometime after the magazine you so kindly sent me for which please accept many thanks. I am very much pleased with the Magazine but I could not imagine who was good enough to send it to me until I received your letter.

Guy, noting excellent fishing in June, expressed regret that the quest for tarpon had gone so badly in March and suggested that they try again. But not in June.

> I would not advise you to visit this place now for the 'Skeets' are something fearful, and I fear you would never come again if you should once meet our summer visitors in such numbers as there are now.

Guy also reported a strange adventure. He accompanied Bill Burton on a mail run to Key West. On the return trip the boat capsized in eight feet of water, but

> as we worked fast, we managed to save nearly all of our clothing and groceries, as well as the mail bag which we piled on the high side of the boat until help came which was not long, for there were two boats near us when the accident happened, so after freeing the boat of water and getting everything on board once more we continued our way not much the worse for our ducking.
>
> Please give my kindest regards to your Father and Mother, also to Sanford Cluett, when next you write to or see him. With best wishes to yourself I remain, Very truly Your friend.

While Guy was concerned with tarpon fishing, mosquitoes, and capsizing boats, Walter Smith and his son Tom were finding that life was far from peaceful and serene at the Smith house.

One night in late winter the Smiths were sitting relaxing after dinner. They were all there, the captain and Rebecca and their five children, Tom, Mamie, Danny, Ed, and Ruby. Suddenly gunshots rang out. Bullets poured through the flimsy walls.[5]

"Hit the floor," the captain shouted.

They all lay flat, trembling in fear as the bullets whistled through above them.

Then the gunfire ceased and all was quiet again, the only sound the crying of the smaller Smith children. The captain edged the door open and peered out into the darkness. No one was there. Just as he expected. It had to be Uncle Steve's gang, Smith figured.

To the Smiths the gunfire could have only one message: Get out of town.

Smith was not an introspective man. He promptly sailed the *Cleveland* across to Key West. He had a purchase he wanted to make. When he returned to Flamingo, he was armed with a powerful rifle, a brand-new Winchester .38.

There was no turning back now for Walter Smith. Blood enemies, that was how he saw the Roberts clan and all their hangers-on. That even included his old friend from Lantana, Guy Bradley. Guy used to be a friend of the Smith family. No more. Now Guy was a friend of those wild Roberts boys, and even Uncle Steve himself. Where it would lead, Walter Smith didn't know. But one thing he did know. He wasn't going to back down.

20 Shootout at Oyster Keys

To the south, Florida Bay lay flat and still, a pale vista broken only by small islands floating in the shimmering heat of a July morning.

Suddenly the sound of gunfire shattered the morning quiet. Guy Bradley stepped out the front door. He squinted and looked out across the bay. Just beyond the island in front of his home lay Oyster Keys, two small islands about two miles away. A blue schooner was anchored near the keys. Guy recognized it even at two miles—the *Cleveland*.[1]

Guy knew what he had to do. And he knew he had to do it alone. Two deputy wardens he could have called on, his brother and his brother-in-law, were both away. Guy got his .32-caliber pistol, walked down to the water, and tried to launch his small sailboat. But there was no wind. The *Audubon* was not in operation. He would have to row the dinghy.

Fronie was there at the water's edge to tell him good-bye. There was tension and fear in the air. Fronie also recognized the boat that lay off Oyster Keys. She watched Guy row out into the bay. Then she went back into the house. It was nine o'clock, the morning of July 8, 1905.

"Ma, can I have some bread?" asked almost-five-year-old Morrell Bradley.

"Wait till your father comes back."

Little Ed Smith was playing near the beach in front of his house. He saw Guy Bradley row past on his way to Oyster Keys. Ed was only eight, but he understood what was happening. He looked across the water with a feeling of dread. His father and his brothers Tom and Danny were all out there on the *Cleveland*.[2]

From the deck of his schooner Walter Smith saw Bradley approaching. There was nothing to do but wait him out. At low tide the *Cleveland* was stuck on a mud bank. Smith fired a warning shot into the air, a signal to his two sons to stop shooting cormorants and return to the schooner.

The two boys fired once more into the rookery, in full view of the warden, then climbed aboard the boat carrying two cormorants. Below in the boat's cabin were Frank Eldridge, who lived with the Smiths, and Alonzo Baker of Key West. Baker had wanted to go turtle hunting on one of the keys east of Flamingo. At Oyster Keys the boat had stopped to let Tom and Danny shoot "a mess of birds" in the rookery while Captain Smith waited for high tide.

Walter Smith's was the only eyewitness version of what happened that day.[3]

"I want your son Tom," Bradley called out, according to Smith.

"Well, if you want him, you have to have a warrant."

"I don't need one," Bradley replied. "I saw them shoot into the rookery and I see the dead birds. Put down your gun, Smith."

"You are one of those fellows who shot into my house and I'll not put down my gun when you are near me. If you want him, you have got to come aboard this boat and take him," Smith said, picking up his .38-caliber Winchester.

"Put down that rifle and I will come aboard," said Guy.

Then, Smith said, Guy cursed him and fired at him with his pistol. Tom dived into the cabin and Danny hit the deck. The shot was wild, hitting the mast, according to Smith. The sharpshooter ducked behind the mast and fired down at Bradley with his Winchester.

"He never knew what hit him," Smith said later. Bradley fell forward in the bow. The dinghy drifted off toward the west.

The Smith party waited aboard the grounded *Cleveland* for what must have seemed an eternity. Finally high tide arrived, and the schooner was free. Smith sailed to Flamingo, arriving about 11 A.M.

He told his family, "We've got to load up and get out of here. I'm going to Key West to give myself up. I've killed Guy Bradley."

That night Guy did not come home. Fronie was used to Guy being away overnight at the rookeries or at Key West, but she knew this night was different. It should have been easy to rejoin his family for supper. Oyster Keys was just two miles away.

Fronie was afraid. It was Captain Smith's schooner she had seen out near the islands, and Smith was the man who had threatened to kill Guy. She had heard gunshots that morning from around Oyster Keys, but then nothing across the afternoon. Now it was night and Smith's boat was gone. And still Guy was missing.

She slept poorly. The next morning she awoke to the sound of rain, dreary and depressing. Fronie called on the Roberts family to help her.[4]

"I'll look for him, Fronie," said Gene.

Gene Roberts, who sometimes worked as Guy's deputy, sailed out into the drizzling rain. If Guy had run into trouble at Oyster Keys, he would have been carried west by the current, somewhere out toward East Cape Sable.

Later that morning he sighted Guy's little boat, drifting aimlessly in the distance. Not a good sign, thought Gene. He drew closer to the boat and still saw no signs of life. It had drifted almost to Sawfish Hole, where a small village of Negroes lived. Finally Gene caught up with the little craft.

Guy lay dead in the bottom of the boat. A bullet had gone completely through his body and come out in back. His revolver lay beside him. "Just as though it had fallen out of his hand," said Gene.

Roberts sailed back to Flamingo for help. He dreaded breaking the news to Fronie and the children. And to Guy's brother, Lou. Guy's parents were away in Miami, where Lydia Bradley, already in poor health, was seeing a doctor. Maggie, Guy's sister, would have to be told, as would Bill Burton, away in Key West picking up the mail for the little village.

Gene rounded up his brother Loren, one of Guy's closest friends. The Roberts brothers, Frank Irwin, and the coroner, Judge Lowe, set out for Sawfish Hole.

Judge Lowe examined Guy's wound. The bullet had entered at the collarbone and had exited in the back, shattering two vertebrae. The judge did what he could to conduct a makeshift coroner's inquest. The Roberts brothers meanwhile had located some cypress boards that were on hand for boat construction. They began building a coffin.

As Guy Bradley's burial site the brothers picked East Cape Sable, the southernmost point on the mainland of the United States, the end of the line in every sense of the word. A serenely beautiful spot, isolated and unspoiled.

The Roberts boys and Irwin dug the grave and lowered Guy into it in his cypress coffin. It was a simple grave, near the only other grave on the cape. That grave held the body of a little Flamingo boy who had died of snakebite when he fell into a nest of cottonmouth moccasins.

21 No True Bill

"I'VE SHOT GUY BRADLEY," Smith told Sheriff Frank Knight. "I don't know whether he's dead or just badly injured." But Smith had already told his own family that Guy was dead.

The sheriff took him into custody and then called in state senator W. Hunt Harris, newly named as the prosecuting attorney. Harris, who had helped pass and later save the law that created Bradley's position, recommended that Smith be held until evidence could be secured.

Sheriff Knight made plans to visit Flamingo to learn the findings of the coroner's jury. By this time the authorities had word that Guy was dead. Judge Beverly Whalton set bail at five thousand dollars and ordered Baker and Eldridge held as accessories and the Smith boys as material witnesses.

Baker, a Key West property owner, was released on his own recognizance. He offered to bail Smith out. The old captain declined.

"If I got out, there would just be more shooting. It'd be me against the Robertses. I don't want any more killing."

Word spread quickly around Key West.[1] Both Smith and Bradley were widely known figures in the county seat. Bill Burton, in Key West to pick up the Flamingo mail, heard the terrible news. He steadied himself, then set about trying to do what little he could. He started by asking the advice of Mayor George Bartlum and attorney Louis A. Harris, the lawyer who had been a friend of Guy's. Louis was a cousin of the prosecutor, Hunt Harris.

Next, Burton went to J. W. Atkins's telegraph office and wired Dutcher of Bradley's death. He told the Audubon president he would like to hire Louis Harris to help with the prosecution of Smith.

A stunned Dutcher wrote back on July 22, authorizing Burton to employ Harris. He also requested detailed information on the case.

The attorney responded with a letter that condemned Smith in the harshest of terms:

Smith sent for me and requested that I visit him in the Jail. He then requested me to defend him, stating that he could raise whatever fee I should charge. I told him that Guy Bradley was a personal friend of mine and that the prosecution would suit me better. He insisted upon giving me his version of the case, after being warned by me that anything he should state might be used against him.

He stated that on the 8th inst he together with his two sons and Alfonso Baker and a man named Eldridge were in his schooner, *Cleveland,* near the Bird Rookery in front of Flamingo, that the wind was very light so that the schooner could not make headway and that his sons Tom and Dan went into the rookery to shoot a mess of birds.

That after they had fired a few shots in the Rookery, he observed Guy Bradley coming out in his small sailboat. That he, Smith, having a rifle, immediately fired a shot as a signal for his boys to return from the Rookery. The boys then came out of the Rookery and fired a shot in the open in plain view of Bradley and came towards the schooner, arriving about five minutes before Bradley, having with them two dead cormorants in their boat.

The warden (Harris's letter continued) told Smith he wanted his son Tom. Smith demanded to see a warrant, but Bradley told him it was not necessary. Words followed and then, Smith said, Guy cursed him and fired his pistol at him.

> Smith says that as soon as the smoke cleared from Bradley's pistol he shot at him with the rifle and that Bradley fell down in the bow of his boat, rallied and raised up on his knees and taking his pistol in both hands tried to fire it again, but was too weak and fell back in the boat.

Smith's story was, to a certain extent, corroborated by his two sons, Harris wrote, but not by Baker and Eldridge, who were below decks. They had heard angry conversation but had not seen the shooting.

Harris went on to point out that Smith had killed a law enforcement officer who was making an arrest. He also observed several discrepancies in Smith's story.

> Of course, Smith's plea is self defense but his own story does not show that he was not to blame, and before he can set up self defense he must show that he

was not to blame in bringing on the difficulty, particularly as he killed an officer of the law engaged in the discharge of his duty.

Bradley was found dead in his boat, near Bowman Landing, the morning of the 9th. A rifle ball had entered his right breast high up, near the shoulder and ranging downward and on a diagonal had pulverized about four inches of his backbone in the region of the last or floating ribs. It was proven at the preliminary hearing that Bradley was a very left-handed man and always shot with his left hand. So it strikes me, as a strong circumstance that he was not trying to shoot Smith when Smith shot him, or he would have been shot in the left side. Also medical experts claimed that after Bradley was shot he could not have gotten to his knees as Smith says.

Harris also quoted Uncle Steve Roberts, who contended that Smith had previously threatened to kill Bradley if he ever again made an attempt to arrest him—proof, Harris said, that malice aforethought existed.

If Smith will tell before a jury on his trial the same story he told at the preliminary hearing under proper instructions on the law he ought to be convicted of murder in one of its degrees, or of manslaughter.

In my opinion, it was a cold-blooded murder, and he deliberately sent his boys into that Rookery for the purpose of enticing Bradley out for the purpose of killing him.

Harris followed that remarkable charge with a paragraph, tossed off almost as a throwaway thought, that should have set off alarm bells from Key West to Manhattan:

At the preliminary hearing Senator W. Hunt Harris defended Smith and put up a very strong fight.

Senator W. Hunt Harris, attorney for the defense? Senator Harris, who a week earlier had been the prosecuting attorney? Senator Harris, one of the most powerful figures in Monroe County and, for that matter, in the state. Within two years he would be named president of the Florida state senate.

Captain Smith had made a brilliant move. He, or his connections in Key West, had enlisted in his cause the prosecution and, in effect, the power structure of Monroe County.

Word of the tragedy was slow in coming out of Key West. Guy's parents were living aboard the *Pearl* in Biscayne Bay when the story appeared in the *Miami Metropolis* on July 14, six days after the shooting. The Reverend E. V. Blackman, like E. R. Bradley an employee of the Model Land Company, saw the story in the paper. He knew the Bradleys had not yet heard of their son's death. He cabled Key West for more information, then broke the sad news to them. Two of the Bradley daughters had already died, and now their son Guy had been murdered.

Edwin Bradley talked with a reporter from the *Miami Metropolis.* He told him his son had had a great deal of trouble with violators of the game laws.

"Was Smith one of these violators?" the reporter asked.

"Yes, Captain Smith, in particular, was in the habit of breaking the laws."

Fronie had little time for grief. Her days were filled with the task of caring for two small children, Morrell, five, and Ellis, two. To help her across those trying days her brothers, Shelly and Almon Vickers, came over from Key West.

One night in July the two brothers decided they would no longer wait for the slow and uncertain wheels of justice. They went to the Smith house. Some blacks had moved in after the Smiths abandoned it. The Vickers boys ordered them out. Then they set the house on fire, destroying along with it all the Smiths' furniture, including a piano that no one played.[2]

Later, under oath, many of the townspeople would swear they were unaware of the fire until after the fact. Actually, the whole town knew. Many helped the Vickers brothers, and nearly all the townspeople were cheering them on.

After the fire Uncle Steve Roberts, Smith's implacable foe, became the proud owner of one of the captain's most prized possessions, his horse.

Dutcher studied Harris's letter carefully. It established clearly that Guy was killed in the line of duty. He was shot while attempting to arrest a poacher whose father freely admitted that illegally killed birds were still in his son's hands at the moment Guy arrived at Smith's schooner. The Audubon leader concluded that the widest possible publicity must be given to the Guy Bradley story. Dutcher summarized Harris's account for the major New York papers. Detailed stories ran in the *New York Times,* the *New York Herald,* the *New York Sun,* the *New York American,* the *Philadelphia North American,* and George Grinnell's widely read weekly *Forest and Stream.* And, of course,

the official Audubon publication, *Bird Lore,* and the AOU's *The Auk* continued to inform the faithful.

Most people assumed that justice would prevail, that the law would deal
harshly with a man who had killed a lawman in the line of duty. An old Palm
Beach friend of Guy's, Cap Dimick's daughter Belle, wrote:

> He loved the rooks which he was placed there to protect, and patrolled the
> swampy land with never abating enthusiasm and fidelity. A group of rook
> killers concerned in the secret traffic of bird plumage shot him in order to kill as
> many birds as they liked. They succeeded, and only one of the band has yet
> been caught. He, it is pleasant to note, will suffer the full penalty of the Florida
> law. "And let fowl multiply in the earth," said the Book of Books—and it is not
> untimely to remember then an ancient injunction today, when the feathered
> folk are in such severe danger at the hands of our women of fashion and their
> cat's paws, the hatmakers.

A note of caution appeared, however, in a letter sent to the national association by Morris K. Jesup, president of the New York Audubon Society.
Prophetically he warned: "Justice may be defeated if the case is left to the
county officials, and it is imperative that this Society shall employ the best
legal talent to be found to see that the majesty of the law is upheld and that
Walter Smith shall receive his just desserts for the unnecessary, unwarranted
and brutal murder of Guy M. Bradley."

Dutcher took the advice of Jesup. He replaced his local lawyer, Louis Harris, with Colonel James T. Sanders of Miami. The colonel was a highly regarded member of the bar, well known in the thriving, bustling new towns of
Miami, Palm Beach, and West Palm Beach. But Key West, bigger in population than all the southeast coastal cities combined, was not new. It was an old
fishing town, and an island at that. Usually out-of-towners are out of their element in a closed society like Monroe County. It was a world that the idealis-
tic William Dutcher in faraway, structured urban New York City was totally
incapable of understanding—and so, apparently, was Colonel Sanders.

Captain Smith sat in his jail cell awaiting the action of the grand jury. A hearing had been scheduled for November. Now it was postponed for another
month. He was already an old man, nearly seventy, when he entered the jail in

July. Feelings of guilt, fear of the noose, and months of incarceration were aging him rapidly. His eyesight, so keen when he served the Confederates as a sharpshooter four decades earlier, began to fail him in the darkness of his Key West cell.

Will they hang me? he wondered. It was self-defense, he kept telling himself. Anyone could see that. A man has to stand up for his family's honor, a man has to look out for his son. They try to claim I killed a deputy sheriff trying to make an arrest. He wasn't no sheriff, just a bird warden. Just a bird warden trying to enforce a law nobody believes in anyway. Besides, he was one of that Roberts gang that shot up my house. It was him or me.[3]

On December 8, 1905, five months after the shooting, the Monroe County grand jury met. Hunt Harris, who knew better than anyone else how the county worked, had done his job well. He realized there was no sympathy in Key West for the law Guy had been enforcing, so how serious could a violation of that law be? When the long-delayed case finally went to the grand jury, the prosecution made no more than a halfhearted effort to secure an indictment, calling just one witness against Smith, Uncle Steve Roberts.

Discrepancies in Smith's story went unchallenged, Colonel Sanders reported to Dutcher. The captain had claimed that Bradley shot first, yet, Sanders said, the position of its firing pin indicated that Guy's pistol had not been fired. Furthermore, he claimed, all six of its bullets were still in the firing chamber.

Of all Smith's defenses, the one that impressed the jurors most was his statement that Bradley in firing first had hit the *Cleveland*'s mast. To back up his contention, he had pointed out to the sheriff what appeared to be a bullet hole high on the mast. Sanders fumed later that no effort had been made to inspect the hole to see if it contained a bullet.

Other unanswered questions were: Why didn't Sanders challenge the holes in Smith's defense? Why didn't he find out if there was a bullet hole in the mast? And if so, why didn't he investigate to see if it did contain a .32-calibre bullet?

"No true bill." That was the finding of the Monroe County grand jury.

By day's end, the killer of Guy Bradley was a free man.

22 The Fight Goes On

WHEN AUDUBON WAS incorporated on January 5, 1905, as the National Association of Audubon Societies, it was led by Dutcher as president and T. Gilbert Pearson as secretary. Pearson, who had spent his childhood at Archer, Florida, had organized and headed an active Audubon Society in North Carolina. He once wrote, "The surest way to send a wild bird into oblivion is to set a price on its head."

After the death of Bradley, the organization's leaders threw their support behind an effort to help Fronie Bradley and the two little boys, Morrell and Ellis. Dutcher's appeal for contributions to the Mrs. Bradley Fund appeared in *Bird Lore*:

> The sad and shocking death of this young woman's breadwinner has left her with two young children to care for. His death, occurring while in the employment of this Society, and while in the discharge of his duties, makes the Association morally if not legally obligated to give the widow and children help....
>
> Bradley gave his life that the cause of bird protection should be perpetuated. All who desire to have our great movement continued can do no less than to see that the wife and children of the first martyr to the cause shall have suitable care or at least a home given them in a place where the mother can support the children.

To start the fund rolling, such well-known leaders in the world of ornithology as William Brewster, Frank Chapman, Morris Jessup, and Dutcher contributed to Mrs. Bradley's aid. The largest single contribution to the fund was $225, given in Guy's memory by the Reverend H. K. Job. The money was the exact amount paid to Job by *Collier's* magazine for his story "Bird Protection's First Martyr." The Audubon Society was delighted with the contribution the story had produced. Within two years they would be less than delighted at complications created by Job's article.

From Florida, Fronie Bradley wrote to Dutcher: "I am at my mother's in Key West. . . . I take in sewing, quilting, and fancy work, and make two or three dollars a week. My children are too small to help, as one is five years old and the other two years."

For a while Fronie toyed with the idea of using the money to buy a chicken farm. Then as contributions approached $1,800, she changed her mind. She decided on a home in Key West.

In April 1906, Gilbert Pearson returned to the state where he lived as a child to perform what his biographer, Oliver H. Orr Jr., described as a four-fold mission: "to visit bird reservations in Tampa Bay, to look for bird colonies on government islands that could be made reservations, to investigate egret plume trade, and to buy a house in Key West for Mrs. Guy Bradley, the martyred warden's widow."[1]

Although he found a number of "Tricolored Herons and Brown Pelicans," he found fewer than a dozen "Egrets and Snowy Herons" in a six-week trip along the Florida west coast. He also found Floridians not overly sympathetic to the egrets' cause, since the plume birds were not regarded as "effective destroyers of obnoxious insects."

After his return, Pearson wrote an eloquent plea for the cause: "The pure glossy whiteness of their plumage and the elegance of their form and movement are sufficient reasons for preserving these living objects of statuary of the southern marshes, even as civilized man preserves in the home and in the forum the marble statues, carved by the hands of inspired artists."

When Pearson arrived in Key West aboard the two-masted sailing vessel he had chartered, he stepped in the loop of a rope and was jerked overboard. He suffered a dislocated shoulder and two broken ribs.

The Audubon secretary was able, however, to escort Fronie on a tour of houses for sale in Key West. For a price of $1,499.08 Guy's widow purchased "a very comfortable house and a lot 40 x 30 feet." The roomy two-story house with large front porches upstairs and down was located on Newton Street. A continuing fund of $400 was set aside for the Bradley family, based on the money eventually collected.

Disheartened by the failure of Monroe County to bring the killer to justice, Audubon made no effort to replace Guy. His old job as warden went unfilled. Frank Chapman commented:

> I don't think those people there are worse than anybody else, any more lawless, or any more dishonest. It is simply a question of no law enforcement. There is no law enforcing body in Flamingo; no police, no courts nearer than Key West, ninety miles away by water, no mail routes even. . . . In such a condition as that each man is the regulator of his own conduct. There is nothing to constrain him to obey the laws if he doesn't want to. Egret plumes are now worth double their weight in gold. There is no community sufficiently law-abiding to leave a bank vault unmolested if it were left unprotected. This is just the same. We have given up. We can't protect it and the rookery will have to go.[2]

Mrs. Marrs was equally downcast. "The subject of providing game wardens is a serious one," she said. "Few responsible men after the murder of Guy M. Bradley are willing thus to jeopardize their lives, for, if the laws of the state cannot be enforced and criminals brought to justice, no man has a guarantee for his safety."

Mrs. Marrs proved all too right. As warden of DeSoto County, Columbus McLeod patrolled the area around Charlotte Harbor and the lower Peace River. On October 1, 1908, he reported to Audubon a thousand curlew, 500 pelicans, 250 cormorants, and 150 cranes. He also reported a decrease in plume birds, due, he felt, to shooting by tourists and native fishermen for food and for mounting by taxidermists.

Wrote McLeod: "I protected this Sunset Island Colony for three years in my feeble way without a cent of compensation except the love I had for the wild, free birds and the pleasure it gave me to save the lives of every single bird that I could. Since that time you have engaged me as a warden for the Audubon Societies with a salary and a nice little boat which enable me to look after their interests more and give them better protection."

Within a month McLeod and his Audubon patrol boat turned up missing. In mid-December his boat was found, weighted down by two heavy sacks of sand and sunk in Charlotte Harbor. In the boat police found the warden's hat with two long gashes in the crown, apparently cut with an axe. In the cuts were bits of hair, and blood was found in the boat.

Investigators concluded he had been sunk with the boat but had floated free and been carried out into the Gulf of Mexico, where sharks would have disposed of his remains. McLeod's body was never found, no arrests were ever made, and no convincing motive has ever been advanced for the murder. It was believed, though, that his bird protection duties probably led to his death. Police ruled out robbery. The *Punta Gorda Herald* on December 17, 1908, advanced a bizarre motive. The paper pointed out that he had been living as a hermit on an island called Cayo Polau, one of the islands rumored to hold pirate's treasure. Could he have been killed for a treasure he was guarding? The Audubon Society would probably have answered the *Herald* that the birds of plume were a Florida treasure.[3]

In the same year that McLeod was apparently murdered, Pressly Reeves, an employee of the South Carolina Audubon Society, was shot to death from ambush near Branchville. A prosperous young farmer, Reeves was driving his wagon home when he was killed by a full charge of buckshot. His mules continued their return to the farmhouse, where his father discovered his body in the wagon. Bloodhounds failed to pick up the trail of the assassins. There were suspects, two fish pirates who had repeatedly threatened Reeves for his active role in destroying illegal fish traps. No arrests were ever made.

Despite three warden murders in three years, Audubon was not about to surrender to the plume trade. Propaganda was directed relentlessly at the wearers of the hats, at the manufacturers, and at the merchants. Ever heavier pressure was brought to bear on state legislatures and on Congress to pass laws restricting the killing of birds, the movement of plumes across state lines, and the importation of feathers.

Meanwhile, Walter Smith continued to plague the Audubon Society. After his release from the Monroe County jail, Smith and his family had little left— no house, no money, just the *Cleveland*.[4] They sailed first to Chokoloskee, where they eked out a hard and meager living harvesting clams. Then, remembering an area he had liked when he first moved to Lantana, Smith sailed around Cape Sable and up the east coast to the Hillsboro Inlet, where the barefoot mailman Ed Hamilton had died. He maneuvered on into Lettuce Lake and Cypress Creek, where Guy and Louie and Charlie Pierce had hunted plume birds on the first leg of the cruise of the *Bonton*.

There in the farming village of Pompano he settled down and began farming. When Pompano was incorporated in 1908, its first mayor, ironically, was Judge John Mizell, Steve Roberts's uncle.

In 1907 a New York lawyer, Herbert Limburg, acting on Smith's behalf, entered a lawsuit against *Collier's* and against the *New York American* for stories they had printed during the period between Smith's arraignment and his release from jail. The puzzling question is how any connection could have been made between Smith in a remote farming village and the respected Limburg, a member of the eminent Lehman family. One explanation is that the Milliners' Association saw a possibility for further harassing the Audubon forces.

Each publisher was sued for $50,000 in libel damages. Since Smith was never convicted, it was clear that the unwary use of words like "murderer" was libelous. The only real question was what his reputation was worth. The case dragged on for three years before a jury returned a verdict in the *Collier's* case. Smith had sought $50,000; he was awarded $750 plus court costs of $208.50. The *American* settled out of court, probably for a similar amount.[5]

"The lawyers took all of it, anyway," Smith complained bitterly. "But at least I proved my point. A jury ruled in my favor in Key West, and people said it was because people there were lawless, frontier types. But we won in the biggest city in the country, too. They even had six niggers on the jury."[6]

Smith lived on until January 5, 1935. When he died, people had forgotten he had anything to do with Guy Bradley. The story of his death made the first page of the *Fort Lauderdale News*, but not because he killed Bradley. Indeed, the story made no mention of the killing. Smith was front-page news because he was the last surviving Confederate veteran in Broward County.

Tom Smith, whose youthful excesses brought on the fatal confrontation, turned to law enforcement, serving on the police force of Pompano.

The E. R. Bradleys and the Burtons moved away from Flamingo after Guy's death. Lou stayed on, living with Gene Roberts and his family. Guy's house and land were bought by his old friend Loren Roberts. Gene Roberts met with Smith in Miami and bought his Flamingo land for forty dollars. In December of 1913 Guy's mother succumbed to cancer, and two years later his father died near Homestead, Florida, where he had been living with the Burtons.

Since 90 percent of all aigrettes were sold in New York State, Pearson, as secretary of the National Association, registered as a lobbyist and went to work on the New York legislature, meeting at Albany. The goal of Pearson was legislation restricting the importation of plumes into the state where the hats were produced. The milliners and the Feather Importers' Association of New York fought the bill bitterly. They contended that twenty thousand workers would be thrown out of work and investments of seventeen million dollars would be lost. The bill passed overwhelmingly in the house, then went to the state senate, where it had strong support. It passed with only three dissenting votes a little less than five years after the death of Guy Bradley. Within the year William Dutcher suffered a severe stroke that left him paralyzed and virtually helpless. Pearson took charge of the organization, and on January 4, 1911, the board of directors gave him the status of chief executive officer—but not the title of president. That title remained with Dutcher until his death on July 1, 1920. Later that year Pearson was elected president.[7]

Important federal legislation further tightened the controls on the importation of plumes into the United States, and the feather trade dried up little by little, undermined further by changes in fashion. In Florida it lingered until World War II, kept alive in part by Bradley's old friends Gene and Loren Roberts, who sold plumes to the wealthy sport Billy Burdine, heir to a department store fortune. As a lark Burdine, at the wheel of his high-powered motorboat, whisked his illegal cargo from the Ten Thousand Islands over to Havana for resale in Paris.[8]

Then, on December 8, 1951, forty-six years to the day after a Monroe County grand jury released Walter Smith, an event occurred in Key West that would have brought a smile of satisfaction to the ghost of Guy Bradley. A six-man criminal court jury returned a guilty verdict against two Chokoloskee men charged with killing white ibis—and assaulting Henry Bennett, the Audubon warden who arrested them. The judge fined them one hundred dollars each and gave them suspended six-month jail sentences. The prosecutor was Allen B. Cleare. Guy and Fronie had bought groceries from his father.[9]

But Guy Bradley was not yet at peace. In September of 1960 Hurricane Donna smashed into Cape Sable. One of her victims was Cuthbert Rookery. The wild, remote treasure island that once excited the wildest greed of the plume hunters was virtually destroyed, not shot out but wiped out by nature.

Another of Donna's victims was the grave of Guy Bradley with its plaque lovingly placed there more than fifty years earlier by Florida Audubon. It read:

GUY M. BRADLEY

1870–1905

FAITHFUL UNTO DEATH

AS GAME WARDEN OF MONROE

COUNTY HE GAVE HIS LIFE FOR

THE CAUSE TO WHICH HE WAS

PLEDGED

ERECTED BY THE FLORIDA AUDUBON SOCIETY

Fortunately, the plaque was later recovered by a park employee and its message made a part of the museum in the Flamingo Visitors Center of Everglades National Park. And on the grounds just outside the building, a larger memorial was erected by the Tropical Audubon Society of Miami. Its tribute to Guy Bradley reads:

AUDUBON WARDEN WAS SHOT AND

KILLED OFF THIS SHORE BY OUTLAW

FEATHER HUNTERS, JULY 8, 1905.

HIS MARTYRDOM CREATED NATIONWIDE

INDIGNATION, STRENGTHENED BIRD

PROTECTION LAWS AND HELPED BRING

EVERGLADES NATIONAL PARK

INTO BEING

ERECTED IN HIS MEMORY BY

THE TROPICAL

AUDUBON SOCIETY

Notes

Chapter 1. The Feather Trade

1. In Africa, legend claims that elephants go to special places to die, which means any poacher finding an elephants' graveyard would reap untold wealth in tusks, just as a plume hunter finding the last great rookery in Florida would become a rich man.

2. According to the entry by Amanda Aaron in *The Encyclopedia of New York City*, edited by Kenneth T. Jackson (Yale University Press: New Haven, 1995), the name Ladies' Mile "applied to a shopping district along Broadway and Sixth Avenue that took form in the mid nineteenth century, as wealthy residents of lower Manhattan moved north. The anchor of the district was the store of R. H. Macy, which opened in 1858 at Sixth Avenue and Fourteenth Street, near wealthy customers who lived on Fifth Avenue. During the next twenty years other stores followed, marking off a district between the stores of A. T. Stewart at Ninth Street and Stern Brothers at Twenty-third Street.... Commercial establishments such as publishers and booksellers gradually replaced the residences on Fifth Avenue, and by the time of the First World War the Ladies' Mile had been abandoned by department stores for sites farther north."

3. Accounts of Chapman's bird count can also be found in Doughty, *Feather Fashions and Bird Preservation*; Ossa, *They Saved Our Birds*; and Welker, *Birds and Men*.

4. Owing to its quiet action, the Flobert rifle was considered ideal for plume hunting, but because of its lack of firepower it was not held in high regard by the Sears, Roebuck catalogue for 1900. Sears sold a $1.60 Flobert but warned: "Buy a good rifle. It will pay in the end."

5. The millinery industry in America is covered informatively in Doughty, *Feather Fashions and Bird Preservation*; Pearson, *Adventures in Bird Protection*; Orr, *Saving American Birds*; Welker, *Birds and Men*; and Graham, *The Audubon Ark*.

6. A whimsical title, *Petals Plucked from Sunny Climes,* and a whimsical pen name, Silvia Sunshine, add even further to the charm of this book about a journey through Florida in the 1870s by a mysterious woman whose real name was Abbie M. Brooks.

7. Graham, *The Audubon Ark*, contains excellent summaries of the events of 1886, the pivotal year for America's bird protection movement.

8. The teenage plume hunting ventures of Guy Bradley are described in the Pierce manuscript, the work of Charles W. Pierce, a boyhood friend of the Bradley brothers. The manuscript, housed at the Historical Society of Palm Beach County offices in Palm Beach, was the basis for *Pioneer Life in South Florida,* edited by Donald Curl, and for "The Cruise of the *Bonton*," edited by Charlton Tebeau and published in *Tequesta,* the journal of the Historical Association of Southern Florida.

Chapter 2. The Letter

1. Material on the Bradley family can be found in Linehan, *Early Lantana, Her Neighbors—and More*; Linehan and Nelson, *Pioneer Days on the Shores of Lake Worth*; a short memoir by Louis Bradley, Guy's brother, at the Historical Society of Palm Beach County; and various articles in the *Tropical Sun*.

2. The best sources for information on Kirk Munroe are Leonard, *The Florida Adventures of Kirk Munroe,* and Munroe and Gilpin, *The Commodore's Story*.

Chapter 3. A Veritable Tropical Paradise

1. Louis Bradley's reminiscences transcribed for the Historical Society of Palm Beach County in 1951 are a good source of information on the Bradleys, as is Pierce in *Pioneer Life*.

2. Charlie Pierce's sister Lillie Pierce Voss described Lydia Bradley as "saintly," according to her son, the late Dr. Gilbert L. Voss, marine biologist at the University of Miami.

3. Pierce, *Pioneer Life*. Most of this chapter is based on Pierce's writings, published and unpublished.

4. The memorable plume hunt involving Pierce and the two Bradley boys is described at length in the Pierce manuscript. See also McIver, "Plume Hunt on Cypress Creek."

5. Many spellings of the Old Frenchman's name emerge in various accounts. The author has elected to use "Chevelier" since that is the one that has survived as the name of a bay on Monroe County's west coast and a Florida land company.

6. The Frenchman's exploits are discussed at length in Bethel, *Bethel's History of Pinellas Point*; Tebeau, *Man in the Everglades*; and Scott's articles in *The Auk*.

7. Lettuce Lake, scene of Guy's first big plume hunt, drew its name from large quantities of water lettuce floating on its surface. The lake, located just east of U.S. 1

in Pompano Beach, was renamed Lake Santa Barbara in the 1920s to make its waterfront lots even hotter items in the Florida Land Boom.

Chapter 4. The Cruise of the Bonton

1. The material used in this chapter comes almost entirely from "The Cruise of the *Bonton*," excerpted from the Pierce manuscript and published in the 1962 edition of *Tequesta*. Edited by Charlton Tebeau, "The Cruise" remains to this day the most thoroughly documented account of a Florida plume hunt.

2. Charcoal made by burning buttonwood trunks and limbs was a major source of income for Cape Sable people.

3. From a population of 517 in 1830, Key West grew into Florida's largest city in just sixty years, according to *The Monroe County Environmental Story*, published in 1991 by Monroe County.

4. Kathryn Hall Proby's *Audubon in Florida* traces the artist's travels and work in the state.

5. James A. Waddell of Key West acquired 1,120 acres of Cape Sable land for his coconut plantation, according to Jean Taylor, *Villages of South Dade*.

6. The colorful Gomez shows up not only in the pages of *Forest and Stream* but in such varied Florida books as Marjory Stoneman Douglas's *Everglades*, Gloria Jahoda's *River of the Golden Ibis*, and Karl Grismer's *Story of Fort Myers*.

Chapter 5. The Barefoot Mailman

1. Detailed accounts of the barefoot route are found in Pierce, *Pioneer Life*, and in the lead chapter, "The Barefoot Mailman," of Pratt, *That Was Palm Beach*.

2. For more on the caves, see Pierce, *Pioneer Life*; Munroe and Gilpin, *The Commodore's Story*; and McIver, *Glimpses of South Florida History*: 70.

3. Pratt gave the postal carrier the moniker "the barefoot mailman" in his 1943 novel of the same name, made in 1951 into a Columbia motion picture starring Robert Cummings.

4. The best account of the disappearance of the barefoot mailman is found in Pierce, *Pioneer Life*.

Chapter 6. Tycoons of the Plume Trade

1. Scott's three 1887 articles in *The Auk* provide the information for most of this chapter on the largest plume hunting operation in Florida.

2. The reference here is, of course, to the Old Frenchman, whose name fell victim to many spellings and mispronunciations.

3. Peas Creek today is known as the Peace River, a popular waterway for Florida canoeists.

4. Most of the references to the lively, thriving, but still small town of Fort Myers come from Grismer's *The Story of Fort Myers* and from the *Fort Myers Press*.

5. Information on Batty comes also from *Forest and Stream, The Auk,* and Graham, *The Audubon Ark.* By the end of the 1890s Batty had given up plume hunting and had concentrated on collecting birds and mammals for the American Museum of Natural History—an "honest living," Graham called it.

Chapter 7. Cuthbert's Rookery

1. Accounts of the great rookery in the Everglades appear in Graham, *The Audubon Ark,* and Chapman, *Camps and Cruises of an Ornithologist.*

2. Principal source for the story of George Elliott Cuthbert was his daughter, Cornelia Cuthbert Deas, Perrine postmistress.

3. A patient, thorough man, Cuthbert used a gun with less firepower but one less likely to frighten birds away from the rookery.

4. After Cuthbert returned from Cape Sable, the *Fort Myers Press* reported regularly and respectfully with short items on his activities.

5. Cuthbert's purchase of half of Marco Island for $1,800 was described by his daughter, Cornelia Deas.

6. The *Press* reported also on the tragic fate of Cuthbert's mate, December 10, 1891.

7. A study of the ads in the *Fort Myers Press* shows how important the plume trade was to the little town on the Caloosahatchee and to the newspaper.

8. Half of Marco Island by the early years of the twenty-first century would run into the billions, according to David Kocourek, a realtor on the island since the early days of its development by the Mackle brothers' Deltona Corporation.

Chapter 8. The Palm Beach Dudes

1. The Pierce manuscript provides a rich supply of details about the life of the Bradley family. Pierce's perceptive observations track Guy's maturing past his sickly, tag-along childhood into his increasingly self-reliant teenage years.

2. Guy became a "Palm Beach Dude" before Henry M. Flagler gave the phrase a fancier meaning.

3. The musical career of young Guy Bradley is covered in Charlie Pierce's manuscript, since the two boys learned their skills together.

4. Elisha Newton Dimick understandably preferred to be called Cap, a nickname he acquired as a cap-wearing boy. Ironically, Dimick, a staunch Democrat, became the first mayor of Palm Beach, one of the most Republican of all American cities.

5. The 1889 county election and the flight from Miami is covered in "South Florida Politics," the final chapter of Pierce's *Pioneer Life*.

6. A good account of the arrival of the *Tropical Sun* can be found in Curl, *Palm Beach County*.

7. The county road built by Metcalf marked the end of the days of the barefoot mailman.

8. Guy's mule troubles are covered by both Pierce in his manuscript and Guy's father in the local paper.

Chapter 9. Sharpshooter

1. Davis, *To Appomattox*, provides detailed information on Chimborazo—the Richmond hospital, not the towering volcanic peak in Ecuador.

2. Nearly all the information in this chapter comes from Smith's son Edwin, a respected citizen of Pompano Beach. Deeply concerned with the reputation of his father, he naturally attempted to cast the events of July 8, 1905, in the best possible light.

Chapter 10. Flagler Takes Charge

1. Flagler's early visits to Palm Beach are well documented in three biographies— Martin, *Florida's Flagler*; Chandler, *Henry Flagler*; and Akin, *Flagler*—and in Curl, *Palm Beach County*.

2. The financial dealings of Flagler during his start-up period are covered in detail in the three biographies.

3. For interesting stories on the Celestial Railroad, see Burnett, *Florida's Past*, vol. 3, and Knott, *Palm Beach Revisited*, vol. 2.

4. Pierce, *Pioneer Life*, covers the sad fate of the Cocoanut Grove House.

5. For a balanced discussion of the Styx legend, see Curl, *Palm Beach County*.

6. Chandler, *Henry Flagler*, covers the tycoon's extension of his railroad and hotel empire to Miami in interesting detail.

7. The Model Land Company and its president, James E. Ingraham, who hired Edwin R. Bradley, are both discussed by Chandler.

8. Lauther, *The Lonesome Road,* tells of the Burtons and other early settlers in Linton, which later became Delray Beach.

9. For more on Colonel Bradley, see Curl, *Palm Beach County,* and Knott, *Palm Beach Revisited,* vol. 1.

Chapter 11. The End of the World

1. In addition to his travels among the West Coast rookeries, Scott visited the Cape Sable area to observe the flamingos. See "An Account of Flamingoes."

2. Jean Taylor in her *Villages of South Dade* makes room for the Monroe County village of Flamingo, since its story is closely related to such towns as Homestead, Florida City, and Perrine. Her book includes the story of Duncan Brady.

3. Old settlers like Effie Roberts, widow of Guy Bradley's friend Loren, recalled with amusement the many names of Flamingo.

4. Luther "Buddy" Roberts, Loren's son, is the sole source of this story about the alleged deal between Smith and the Bradley brothers.

5. More information on Harriet Hemenway and her important contribution to the revival of the Audubon movement can be found in Ossa, *They Saved Our Birds,* and Graham, *The Audubon Ark.*

6. Tebeau's *Chokoloskee Bay Country* remains the definitive work on the colorful island.

7. Information on Gregorio Lopez's feather-smuggling scheme comes from a former Audubon warden, Arthur "Bud" Kirk, who passed it on also to Budd Schulberg. The author used the incident in *Wind Across the Everglades,* his 1958 motion picture about plume hunting. The movie was hardly memorable, but Schulberg's introduction to the published version of the script, titled *Across the Everglades,* is highly recommended. For more on *Wind Across the Everglades,* see my book *Touched by the Sun.*

8. Even the exact spelling of Fronie's name is something of a mystery, since the name on her marriage license, written in longhand, appears to be Kirvin but could pass for Kirwin.

Chapter 12. The Patriarch

1. Many of the stories on the Roberts family in Flamingo were related by Effie Roberts, the widow of Loren Roberts.

2. Most of the information on Steve and Dora Roberts during their days in the Orlando area comes from the extensive research files of their grandson Allen R. Taylor of Orlando. Mr. Taylor was kind enough to share his research with Dr. Tebeau and myself.

3. Frederic Remington, one of America's most famous painters of the Old West, came to Florida in 1895 to write and illustrate a story on Florida's "Cracker cowboys" for *Harper's Magazine*. Remington discovered the cowboys were called cow hunters. He also discovered Bone Mizell and made him famous as Remington's *Cracker Cowboy*. For a fuller and highly readable account of the life of this intriguing frontiersman, refer to *Florida Cow Hunter: The Life and Times of Bone Mizell* by Jim Bob Tinsley.

4. The source of this quote is Alexander "Sandy" Sprunt IV, who for many years served as Audubon's vice president and director of research, basing his operation in Tavernier in the Upper Keys. A descendant of America's most distinguished ornithological family, he knew not only the birds but also the colorful people of the Everglades.

5. The story of Gene Roberts's difficult and totally mad scheme came from his sister-in-law Effie Roberts.

6. The discovery of Guy Bradley's initials on the royal palm at Seven Palm Lake was reported in Brookfield and Griswold's *They All Called It Tropical*.

Chapter 13. A Matter of Law

1. An excellent history of the early days of the Audubon Society can be found in *Bird Lore,* January-February 1905, and in a shorter form in Graham, *The Audubon Ark*.

2. For more on the millinery industry, see Doughty, *Feather Fashions and Bird Preservation*; Ossa, *They Saved Our Birds*; Orr, *Saving American Birds*; and Graham, *The Audubon Ark*.

3. *The First One Hundred Years,* published by the Florida Audubon Society, gives an interesting account, not of the society's first century, but rather of its first seventy-five years, adding a few incidents that occurred a few years earlier to justify the title.

Chapter 14. The Badge

1. The story of Fred Whiting, almost too good to be true, comes from the Cracker Historian, Lawrence E. Will, whose book *Okeechobee Catfishing* tells us stories about many colorful lake dwellers.

2. Ed Watson, who could lay claim to the title of Florida's most notorious legend, is discussed in depth in Douglas's *The Everglades,* in Tebeau's books on the Everglades and Collier County, and more recently by Peter Matthiessen in his fictional trilogy *Killing Mister Watson* (1990), *Lost Man's River* (1997), and *Bone by Bone* (1999).

3. The *Blackwood's* code of conduct is presented in Tebeau's *Man in the Everglades.* The somewhat fanciful 1927 article was written under the name Major L.A.M. Jones. The major's claim that four wardens "were murdered, and their bodies found covered with the skins of egrets they had come to protect" was a large exaggeration.

4. Bradley was actually employed by the AOU and to an extent by Monroe County, but the pay of early wardens came from whatever source was willing to help with the funding.

Chapter 15. On the Job

1. Information about the increasing animosity between Walter Smith and the extended Bradley and Roberts families comes from court records of two libel cases Smith brought in 1907 against *Collier's* magazine and the *New York Sun*; from Effie Roberts, widow of Loren Roberts; and from Gilpin, *The Cruise of the Seminole.*

2. Firsthand accounts of Bradley on the job were provided by Job and Bent in their report to Dutcher and in their books, Bent's *Life Histories of North American Birds* and Job's *Wild Wings.*

Chapter 16. A Boat Named Audubon

1. Charlotte Lockwood's *Florida's Historic Indian River County* provides information on the Kroegels, Sebastian, and Barker's Bluff.

2. Excellent accounts of Chapman's visits to Indian River are found in his *Camps and Cruises of an Ornithologist* and Elizabeth Austin's *Frank M. Chapman in Florida.*

3. The birds seem to have inspired a degree of musicality. Bradley and Kroegel both played musical instruments, while Bradley and Chapman were both accomplished whistlers. In addition, Chapman's son became a Metropolitan Opera baritone as well as the husband of a noted Met soprano, Gladys Swarthout.

4. The Sebastian River bridge in 1924 became the scene of the shooting by sheriff's officers of a man who was Florida's most famous outlaw—and also a plume hunter. His name was John Ashley.

5. The problems between Smith and Fred Hurse became part of the record at the *Collier's* libel trial.

6. Flagler's order (see Chandler, *Henry Flagler,* 217) was a significant decision in the history of South Florida, opening up all the Keys as well as Key West to a vast expansion in the years ahead.

Chapter 17. Trouble at Cuthbert

1. The angry exchange between Bradley and Smith was reported to the author by Smith's son Ed.

2. This strange episode came from Sandy Sprunt, narrated with a mixture of amusement and skepticism.

3. Again, Sprunt is the source of this information.

Chapter 18. Life in Flamingo

1. Fronie's boxing prowess was reported by Effie Roberts, whose husband Loren came to grief under the force of Fronie's mighty fists.

2. Ed Smith reported this futile attempt to oust Bradley from his job.

3. Dutcher's visit to Key West to save Guy's job from Smith's trickery is presented in rich detail in the Audubon chairman's journal, preserved now in the New York Public Library.

Chapter 19. Back on the Job

1. Gilpin's fascinating journal was the basis for the book published in 2000 by three of his children. Many years earlier Gilpin had collaborated with Ralph Munroe to write a much revered book on South Florida history, *The Commodore's Story,* published first in 1930 by Ives Washburn. Munroe was the first commodore of the Biscayne Bay Yacht Club and, with Kirk Munroe (not related), cofounder of the club.

2. A company brochure provides an account of Guy's friend's important advance in shirt manufacturing at Cluett, Peabody & Co.

3. Vincent Gilpin's wife, Emma, proved that her husband was not the only family member who could keep an interesting journal.

4. This letter may well have been the last letter Guy wrote to anyone. Thanks to Vincent Gilpin Jr. for permitting its use in this book.

5. Ed Smith provides an eyewitness account of this harrowing episode in the violent, primitive world of Flamingo.

Chapter 20. Shootout at Oyster Keys

1. The morning of July 8, 1905, from the point of view of the Bradley household comes from interviews with Ruby Bradley Whitlock, widow of Morrell Bradley.

2. The Smith version of the same event resulted from talks with Ed Smith, Captain Smith's son who was in the Smith house when Bradley rowed past.

3. Smith's account of the shooting appeared in many Florida and New York newspapers, remaining fairly consistent throughout.

4. Effie Roberts, who came to Flamingo after the death of Bradley, recalled the many discussions of the fateful day both within the Roberts family and among the survivors of Guy Bradley.

Chapter 21. No True Bill

1. The events following the killing of Bradley and the incarceration of Smith were covered in detail in the *Key West Citizen* and the *Miami Metropolis*.

2. Ruby Bradley Whitlock identified the people who burned down Smith's house.

3. Smith's thoughts during his days in the Key West jail were told to the author by his son Ed, who said his father could never forget the events of that year.

Chapter 22. The Fight Goes On

1. Orr's *Saving American Birds* gives a full account of Pearson's trip to Florida to help Fronie Bradley buy her Key West home.

2. Austin's *Frank M. Chapman in Florida* quotes the famous ornithologist's pessimistic remarks to a New York newspaper in 1908.

3. Williams and Cleveland's book on the Charlotte Harbor area, *Our Fascinating Past*, gives a full account of the tragedy of Columbus McLeod.

4. Ed Smith is the source for information on Smith's wanderings following the Bradley murder.

5. Court records provide testimony in the trial. Information on the disposition of the case came from Ed Smith and coverage in the *New York Times*.

6. Walter Smith's bitter quote was recalled by his son.

7. Orr's *Saving American Birds* gives an informative account of Pearson's rise to the presidency of the National Association of Audubon Societies.

8. Billy Burdine's ties to the plume hunting business were well known to Ed Smith and to Effie Roberts. Their recollections indicate that members of the Roberts clan who had worked with Guy Bradley as deputy wardens still pursued the feather trade long after Guy's death.

9. Griswold's *The Florida Keys and the Coral Reef* contains a chapter, "Poachers and Wardens," that details the case of the hunters who had killed white ibis in 1951.

Bibliography

Printed Sources

Akin, Edward N. *Flagler: Rockefeller Partner and Florida Baron.* Kent, Ohio: Kent State University Press, 1988.

American Ornithologists' Union. "Destruction of Our Native Birds." *Science,* November 1886.

Austin, Elizabeth S., ed. *Frank M. Chapman in Florida: His Journals and Letters.* Gainesville: University of Florida Press, 1967.

Bent, Arthur Cleveland. *Life Histories of North American Birds.* Vol. 1, *Water Birds.* Edited and abridged by Henry Hill Collins Jr. New York: Harper, 1960.

Bethel, John. *Bethel's History of Pinellas Peninsula.* 1915. St. Petersburg: Great Outdoors, 1962.

Bradley, Lydia. "Truck Gardening." In *The Lake Worth Historian.* Palm Beach: Ladies of Palm Beach, 1896.

Brookfield, Charles M., and Oliver Griswold. 4th ed. *They All Called It Tropical.* Miami: Data Press, 1957.

Burnett, Gene M. *Florida's Past: People and Events That Shaped the State.* 3 vols. Englewood, Fla.: Pineapple Press, 1986–91.

Burns, Ric, and James Sanders. *New York: An Illustrated History.* New York: Alfred A. Knopf, 1999.

Burrows, Edwin G., and Mike Wallace. *Gotham: A History of New York City to 1898.* New York: Oxford University Press, 1999.

Chandler, David Leon. *Henry Flagler: The Astonishing Life and Times of the Visionary Robber Baron Who Founded Florida.* New York: Macmillan, 1986.

Chapman, Frank M. *Camps and Cruises of an Ornithologist.* New York: Appleton, 1908.

Cruickshank, Helen Gere. *Flight into Sunshine: Bird Experiences in Florida.* New York: Macmillan, 1948.

Curl, Donald W. *Palm Beach County.* Northridge, Cal.: Windsor, 1975.

Davis, Burke. *To Appomattox.* New York: Rinehart, 1959.

Doughty, Robin W. *Feather Fashions and Bird Preservation.* Berkeley and Los Angeles: University of California Press, 1975.

Douglas, Marjory Stoneman. *The Everglades: River of Grass.* New York: Rinehart, 1947.

———. *Nine Florida Stories.* Edited by Kevin M. McCarthy. Jacksonville: University of North Florida Press, 1990.

Flicker, John. "Local Heroes." *Audubon,* November-December 1998.

Fox, Stephen. *John Muir and His Legacy: The American Conservation Movement.* Boston: Little, Brown, 1981.

Fuller, Walter P. "Who Was the Frenchman of Frenchman's Creek?" *Tequesta* 29 (1963).

Gilpin, Vincent. *The Cruise of the Seminole Among the Florida Keys, March 10–April 5, 1905.* West Chester, Pa: 2000.

Graham, Frank. *Man's Dominion: The Story of Conservation in America.* New York: M. Evans, 1971.

Graham, Frank, Jr., with Carl W. Buchheister. *The Audubon Ark: A History of the National Audubon Society.* New York: Alfred A. Knopf, 1990.

Grismer, Karl Hiram. *The Story of Fort Myers.* Facsimile reproduction of 1949 edition. Fort Myers Beach: Island Press, 1982.

Griswold, Oliver. *The Florida Keys and the Coral Reef.* Miami: Graywood Press, 1965.

Hancock, James, and James Kushlan. *The Herons Handbook.* New York: Harper and Row, 1984.

Howell, Arthur H. *Florida Bird Life.* New York: Coward-McCann, 1932.

Huffstodt, James T. *Everglades Lawmen: True Stories of Game Wardens in the Glades.* Sarasota: Pineapple Press, 2000.

Jahoda, Gloria. *River of the Golden Ibis.* New York: Holt, Rinehart and Winston, 1973.

Job, Herbert Keightley. *Wild Wings.* Boston: Houghton Mifflin, 1905.

Kersey, Harry A., Jr. *Pelts, Plumes, and Hides: White Traders Among the Seminole Indians, 1870–1930.* Gainesville: University Presses of Florida, 1975.

Knott, James R. *Palm Beach Revisited.* 2 vols. West Palm Beach: privately printed, 1987–88.

Lauther, Olive Chapman. *The Lonesome Road.* Miami: Center Printing, 1963.

Leonard, Irving. *The Florida Adventures of Kirk Munroe.* Chuluota, Fla.: Mickler House, 1975.

Linehan, Mary Collar. *Early Lantana, Her Neighbors—and More.* St. Petersburg: Byron Kennedy, 1980.

Linehan, Mary Collar, and Marjorie Watts Nelson. *Pioneer Days on the Shores of Lake Worth, 1873–1893.* St. Petersburg: Southern Heritage Press, 1994.

Lockwood, Charlotte. *Florida's Historic Indian River County.* Vero Beach, Fla.: MediaTronics, 1976.

Martin, S. Walter. *Florida's Flagler*. Athens: University of Georgia Press, 1949.

Matthiessen, Peter. *Wildlife in America*. New York: Viking, 1959.

McCally, David. *The Everglades: An Environmental History*. Gainesville: University Press of Florida, 1999.

McIver, Stuart. *Glimpses of South Florida History*. Miami: Florida Flair Books, 1988.

———. "Plume Hunt on Cypress Creek." *Broward Legacy* 1 (October 1976).

———. *True Tales of the Everglades*. Miami: Florida Flair Books, 1989.

Munroe, Ralph Middleton, and Vincent Gilpin. *The Commodore's Story*. 1930. Miami: Historical Association of Southern Florida, 1966.

Orr, Oliver H. Jr. *Saving American Birds: T. Gilbert Pearson and the Founding of the Audubon Movement*. Gainesville: University Press of Florida, 1992.

Ossa, Helen. *They Saved Our Birds: The Battle Won and the War to Win*. New York: Hippocrene, 1973.

Pearson, Thomas Gilbert. *Adventures in Bird Protection*. New York: Appleton-Century, 1937.

Persons, Todd. *The First One Hundred Years*. Maitland, FL. The Florida Audubon Society. 1975.

Pierce, Charles William. "The Cruise of the *Bonton*." *Tequesta* 22 (1962).

———. Manuscript. Historical Society of Palm Beach County, Palm Beach.

———. *Pioneer Life in Southeast Florida*. Edited by Donald Walter Curl. Coral Gables: University of Miami Press, 1970.

Pratt, Theodore. *That Was Palm Beach*. St. Petersburg: Great Outdoors, 1968.

Proby, Kathryn Hall. *Audubon in Florida*. Coral Gables: University of Miami Press, 1974.

Schulberg, Budd. *Across the Everglades*. New York: Random House, 1958.

Scott, William Earl Dodge. "An Account of Flamingoes Observed in the Vicinity of Cape Sable, Florida." *Auk* 7 (1890).

———. "The Present Condition of Some of the Bird Rookeries of the Gulf Coast of Florida." *Auk* 4 (April, July and October 1887).

———. *Story of a Bird Lover*. New York: Outlook, 1903.

Simmons, Glen, and Laura Ogden. *Gladesmen: Gator Hunters, Moonshiners, and Skiffers*. Gainesville: University Press of Florida, 1998.

Sunshine, Silvia. *Petals Plucked from Sunny Climes*. Nashville: Southern Methodist, 1880.

Taylor, Jean. *Villages of South Dade*. St. Petersburg: Byron Kennedy, [1985?].

Tebeau, Charlton W. *Chokoloskee Bay Country*. Coral Gables: University of Miami Press, 1955.

———. *Florida's Last Frontier*. Rev. ed. Coral Gables: University of Miami Press, 1966.

———. *Man in the Everglades*. 2d ed. Coral Gables: University of Miami Press, 1968.

Thompson, Frieda Kroegel. "The Kroegel Family Story." In *Tales of Sebastian,* edited by Arline Westfahl et al. Sebastian, Fla.: Sebastian River Area Historical Society, 1990.

Tinsley, Jim Bob. *Florida Cow Hunter: The Life and Times of Bone Mizell.* Gainesville: University Press of Florida, 1990.

Welker, Robert Henry. *Birds and Men.* Cambridge: Harvard University Press, Belknap Press, 1955.

Wilbanks, William. *Forgotten Heroes: Police Officers Killed in Early Florida.* Paducah, Ky.: Turner, 1998.

Will, Lawrence E. *Lawrence Will's Cracker History of Okeechobee.* St. Petersburg: Great Outdoors, 1964.

———. *A Dredgeman of Cape Sable.* St. Petersburg: Great Outdoors, 1967.

———. *Okeechobee Catfishing.* St. Petersburg: Great Outdoors, 1965.

Williams, Lindsey, and U. S. Cleveland. *Our Fascinating Past: Charlotte Harbor, The Early Years.* Punta Gorda, Fla.: Charlotte Harbor Area Historical Society, 1993.

Manuscript Sources

National Audubon Society Papers. Correspondence and warden reports. New York Public Library.

Pierce, Charles W. Manuscript. Historical Society of Palm Beach County, Palm Beach, Fla.

Interviews

Brookfield, Charles. Personal meetings with author, Miami, 1978.

Buchheister, Carl W. Personal telephone and letter communication with author, New York City, 1979.

Callison, Charles H. Personal telephone and letter communication with author, New York City, 1980.

Deas, Cornelia. Personal meetings with author, Perrine, Fla., 1980.

Huffstodt, James T. Personal meeting with author, West Palm Beach, 1998.

Kirk, Arthur "Bud." Personal meeting with author, Goodland, Fla., 1977.

Roberts, Effie. Personal meetings with author, Florida City, 1977.

Roberts, Luther "Buddy." Personal meeting with author, Florida City, 1992.

Sprunt, Alexander IV "Sandy." Personal meetings with author, Tavernier, Fla., 1978.

Smith, Ed. Personal meetings with author, Pompano Beach, Fla., 1979.

Voss, Gilbert. Personal meetings with author, Miami, 1986.

Whitlock, Ruby Bradley. Personal meetings with author, Key West, 1985.

Will, Lawrence E. Personal meeting with author, Belle Glade, Fla., 1975.

Index

Stuart B. McIver was the author of thirteen books on Florida, nearly 500 magazine articles, and the writer and producer of numerous documentary films, of which *Alligator* won the Venice Film Festival Silver Medal. Both *Alligator* and *Marisa and the Mermaid* won the CINE Golden Eagle award for documentary films.